OSPREY AIRCRAFT OF THE ACES • 8

Corsair Aces of World War 2

SERIES EDITOR: TONY HOLMES

OSPREY AIRCRAFT OF THE ACES • 8

Corsair Aces of World War 2

Mark Styling

OSPREY
AEROSPACE

First published in Great Britain in 1995
by Osprey Publishing, Elms Court, Chapel Way, Botley, Oxford, OX2 9LP

Reprinted 1996, 1998, 1999
© 1995 Osprey Publishing

ISBN 1 85532 530 6

Edited and Chapter Seven by Tony Holmes

Design by TT Designs, Tony & Stuart Truscott

Cover Artwork by Iain Wyllie
Aircraft Profiles by Mark Styling and John Weal
Figure Artwork by Mike Chappell
Scale Drawings by Mark Styling

Printed in Hong Kong

ACKNOWLEDGEMENTS
The author would like to thank the following Corsair pilots for their contributions towards this volume – George C Axtell, Donald L Balch, John F Bolt, Jack Broering, Jim Cupp, Archie Donahue, Marion E Carl, Dewey F Durnford, Roger Conant, Lt Gen Hugh M Elwood USMC(ret), Phillip C Delong, Howard J Finn, Ronnie Hay, Roger Hedrick, J W Ireland, Lt Col Robert M McClurg USMC(ret), Jeremiah J O'Keefe, Edwin L Olander, Bob Owens, Joe D Robbins, Lin Shuman and Kenneth A Walsh. Finally, I would also like to thank William Hess, Peter Mersky, Jim Sullivan and Barrett Tillman for their invaluable assistance. The editor acknowledges the permission of the US Navy FPO for the use of the Solomons campaign map reproduced in chapter one.

EDITOR'S NOTE
To make this new series as authoritative as possible, the editor would be extremely interested in hearing from any individual who may have relevant photographs, documentation or first-hand experiences relating to the elite pilots, and their aircraft, of the various theatres of war. Any material used will be fully credited to its original source. Please write to Tony Holmes at 1 Bradbourne Road, Sevenoaks, Kent, TN13 3PZ, Great Britain.

Front cover
2nd Lt Kenneth Ambrose Walsh, flying F4U-1 'No 13', BuNo 02310, downs his fourth victim and moves onto his next, 15 miles east of the Russell Islands on 13 May 1943. On this day he shot down three Zeros and damaged a fourth, thereby becoming the first Corsair pilot to gain the status of ace. He completed three combat tours in the Solomons, claiming a total of 20 confirmed victories, and he later downed another Zero whilst serving with VMF-222 on Okinawa in 1945. Walsh was the first Corsair ace to be awarded his country's highest award for valour, the Congressional Medal of Honor

CONTENTS

GUADALCANAL DEBUT

The Americans began their offensive against the Japanese South West Pacific perimeter in early 1942. Adm King's plan was to advance step-by-step from Efate, in the New Hebrides, to Espiritu Santo further up the chain. From newly constructed bases the offensive could continue onto the Solomons and the Bismarcks. On 4 April the theatre was split between two commands; Gen Douglas MacArthur took the South West Pacific while Adm Chester Nimitz took command of the Central Pacific. The overall US strategy was that Nimitz's forces would advance upwards across the Pacific island to island, starting in the Gilberts in November 1942, then onto the Marshalls, the Marianas, Iwo Jima and Okinawa. At the same time MacArthur would push north through the Solomons, New Guinea and onto the Philippines.

The key to success in the Solomons campaign was the rapid capture and completion by the Marines of a semi-operational Japanese airfield on Guadalcanal soon after the invasion of 7 August 1942. Ready to accept aircraft by the 12th, it became known as Henderson Field a few days later. Aircraft operating from Henderson and its satellites – 'Fighter Strips One' and 'Two' – were to become known as the 'Cactus Air Force', 'Cactus' being the American code-name for Guadalcanal. The Solomons were to be strongly contested by the Japanese as their loss would place Rabaul under threat – their main bastion of defence in the South Pacific. The Imperial Navy and Army Air Forces therefore committed, and ultimately lost, the bulk of their fully trained units in the defence of the Solomons. The campaign became a defeat from which they would never recover.

The bitter struggle for the Solomons was far from decided when VMF-124, under the command of Maj William E Gise, arrived on Guadalcanal with the Marines' first Chance Vought F4U-1 Corsairs on 12 February 1943. Boasting twice the range of the F4F, the Corsair enabled the hard-pressed 'Cactus Air Force' to attack the Japanese further up the Solomons chain. They were now also able to escort USAAF heavy bombers on long-range strikes, as well as perform sweeps against enemy airfields in the central and northern Solomons.

One of VMF-124's original cadre of pilots sent to the Solomons was Lt Kenneth A Walsh, a determined Marine who was soon to become the first aviator to achieve ace status in the Corsair. Here, he describes VMF-124's combat debut.

'Delivery of the F4U commenced in late October 1942. There were many refinements that had to be

The first prototype XF4U-1 took to the air on 29 May 1940 and a production order was issued on 30 June 1940. The design incorporated the use of the largest and most powerful radial engine of the time, the Pratt and Whitney R-2800, which was to turn the largest propeller ever used on a single-seat fighter. To gain the necessary ground clearance for the prop, Chance Vought incorporated an inverted gull wing which avoided the use of an exceptionally long main undercarriage and had the added bonus of reducing drag. As the wing met the fuselage at roughly right angles, it did not require the usual large fairing associated with the standard design (*via Phil Jarrett*)

This detailed theatre map has been officially produced by the US Navy for its own publications, and clearly shows the central area of operations in and around the Solomons (*reproduced courtesy of the US Navy's FPO office*)

carried out before the planes were combat ready, which delayed our proper conversion to the type. After we gained a complement of 24 aircraft and 29 pilots, we deployed to the Pacific, having only averaged about 20 hours in the F4U. We completed one gunnery hop, an altitude hop, one night flight and then we had to go – they needed us bad. We would have to learn through experience. The F4F Wildcats were out there at Guadalcanal doing a marvellous job of defence, but no way could they

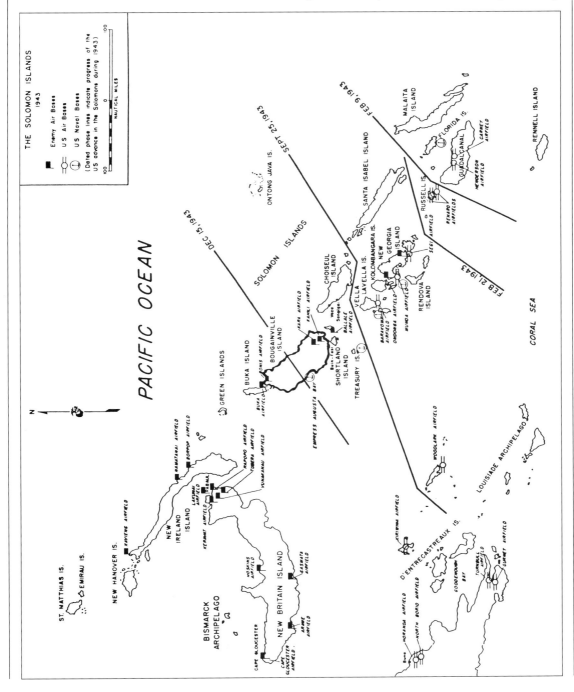

The XF4U-1 on an early test flight. There were major differences between the prototype and the first production aircraft. For example, the armament of one .30 cal and three .50 cal guns was revised to six .50 cal Brownings, three in each wing. The resultant loss in the wing's fuel capacity necessitated the incorporation of a fuel tank forward of the cockpit. This in turn required the cockpit to be moved further aft by three feet, thus worsening forward visibility – to counteract this problem the seat was raised by six inches. Other minor differences included the canopy arrangement and the lack of a tail hook (via Phil Jarrett)

take the offense. The Zero would play with the F4F like a cat with a mouse. The Wildcat also didn't have the range or the combat capability for escort missions. At that time there were only two planes that could do the job – the Corsair and the Army's P-38.

'We deployed in the first week of January 1943. Our 24 F4U-1s went aboard the jeep-carrier *Kitty Hawk*. We went on a cruise liner, rendezvousing with our aircraft at Espiritu Santo in the New Hebrides. We then waited for about 12 days before moving up to Guadalcanal, arriving on 12 February 1943 ready for combat. We took-off early in the morning to fly the 550 miles northwest to the Solomons, escorted by PB4Ys, the Navy version of the B-24. Seventeen F4Us went the first day and the balance followed the next. We landed before noon and immediately we discovered we had been slated for a mission even before we arrived. One hour later we set off from "Fighter Two" strip. The mission was a *Dumbo* escort; protecting a PBY Catalina. Two F4F-4 pilots had been shot down in the Kolombangara area, 200 miles north of Guadalcanal. Having been rescued by coast-watchers, they were moved to Sand Fly Bay, Vella Lavella, from where we were to rescue them. Twelve of our pilots achieved nine hours flight-time that day.

'The two downed pilots we picked up were Lt Jefferson DeBlanc (8 F4F kills) of VMF-112 and SSgt James A Feliton of VMF-121. For the former this was the end of a hair-raising sortie which saw him awarded the Congressional Medal of Honor – DeBlanc had "splashed" five aircraft attempting to dive-bomb Guadalcanal, before being downed himself.

'On the way back the Navy PBY crew also made an unscheduled rescue of an Army P-38 reconnaissance pilot who had ditched off the south coast of New Georgia. During that mission we were only about 50 miles from a large Zero base, and I hesitate to think what might have happened had they known we were coming up – our pilots were so inexperienced and we were at low altitude. We could have lost most, if not all of them, but we lucked out and got them back.

'I had thought that when we got up to the Solomon Islands we would have a chance to familiarise ourselves with the area, ascertaining exactly where Tulagi, Savo, Cape Esperance and the Russells (all the places I'd heard about) were. Not so, as our next mission followed the day after our *Dumbo* sortie! We were to go from Guadalcanal through to Bougainville, 300 miles up "The Slot", escorting B-24s that were to attack Japanese ships in Buin Harbour. I was leading the third four-plane element, and it soon became my usual position to lead the last flight. If there were four flights the aircraft I was flying would be numbered "13". Not being superstitious, from then on I

1st Lt Kenneth Ambrose Walsh prepares for a combat mission. Selected for Naval Flight Training in March 1936, he had experienced seven years of frontline flying before deploying to Guadalcanal with VMF-124 at the age of 26. He became the first Corsair ace, opening his score with two victories on 1 April 1943 (National Archives via Pete Mersky)

would always fly "No 13". During this second mission we again got lucky as only one Zero came out and he just looked us over.

'My first combat mission proper was flown on 14 February as this time the Japanese knew we were coming. Again we were escorting B-24s, but this time they were to hit Kahili aerodrome. The Japanese coast-watchers reported us long before we got there, and the Zeros were waiting when we arrived. We lost our first two pilots that day, along with two B-24s, four P-38s and two P-40s. We got three Zeros in return, one the result of a head-

on collision with one of our F4Us. This, our first introduction to combat, became known as the "St Valentine's Day Massacre". Another similar mission was planned for the next day, but it was cancelled before take-off.

'Being the first unit to go out in the Corsair, we didn't know exactly how to employ it, so we had to establish a doctrine. We knew that there would be many other Corsair squadrons following us, and they would want to know what we did, and how we did it. They would then be able to augment our experience and develop their own tactics. I had asked one very experienced Wildcat pilot, who had made a great name for himself during the early days of Guadalcanal, how to go about combat with the Zero. All he said was "you've gotta' go after them". Well, we knew it would take more than that!

'I learned quickly that altitude was paramount. Whoever had altitude dictated the terms of the battle, and there was nothing a Zero pilot could do to change that – we had him. The F4U could out-perform the Zero in every aspect except slow speed manoeuvrability and slow speed rate of climb. Therefore, you avoided getting slow when combating a Zero. It took time, but eventually we developed tactics and employed them very effectively. When we were accustomed to the area, and knew our capabilities, there were instances when the Zero was little more than a victim. I came to know the Zero, and I learned how to attack it. Being in my seventh consecutive year of frontline flying, I knew how to fire the guns and how to use our Mk 8 gunsight. The guns were boresighted to 1000 ft. The electric sight had rings covering so many mils, 1000 ft equalling one mil. If the Zero covered 40 mils, you knew he was 1000 ft away. We had six .50 cal guns with 400 rounds per gun, and a rate of fire of 800 rounds per minute. Our belt loading was one incendiary, one tracer and one armour piercing. A two-second burst would fire 150 rounds, and the Zero, like most Japanese aircraft, had no armour plating or self-sealing tanks. So, if you hit them, they'd burn, with their aluminium construction including magnesium parts which added further fuel to the fire. You can imagine what would happen if you got 30 or 40 hits on them.

'There were times, however, that I tangled with a Zero at slow speed, one on one. In these instances I considered myself fortunate to survive a

Ken Walsh's 'No 4 Flight', pictured at Guadalcanal in February 1943 at the start of their respective combat careers. Left to right, 1st Lt William Johnston, Jr, 2nd Lt Ken Walsh, 1st Lt Dean Raymond and MSgt Troy Shelton. These pilots would account for the destruction of 27 Japanese aircraft during the Solomons Campaign, Johnston and Raymond claiming two, Shelton three and Walsh twenty. F4U-1 'No 20' shows how VMF-124's aircraft appeared at the start of the tour. The Corsairs were soon repainted with more visible white numbers further aft on the fuselage (*Walsh Collection*)

battle. Of my 21 victories, 17 were against Zeros, and I lost five aircraft as a result of combat. I was shot down three times, and I crashed one that ploughed into the line back at base and wiped out another F4U. I was shot-up at least a dozen times, but usually the aeroplane could be repaired. The times that I really got in trouble came about due to the Zero that I didn't see, and conversely, I'm sure that with most of the kills I got they didn't see me. So, when new units came up behind us

we told them what we had learned. Everything was a calculated risk, but I had a lot more to tell them about than just "you gotta' go after them".

'By July-August 1943 we had eight squadrons in the Solomons equipped with the Corsair. Our first combat tour lasted around seven months – our first mission was on 12 February and the last on 7 September. During that time we destroyed 68 enemy aircraft, but lost some 30 F4Us due to combat and operational causes. Of the 11 pilots lost, three fell in combat and four during operations. One of the pilots killed was our CO, Maj Gise, who was lost during an air battle on 14 May 1943.

'The date of my first kill was 1 April 1943. We were on patrol, going from the Russell's, which were 50 miles north of Patterson Field, to another little island called Baroku, the latter being a good navigational fix from which we could maintain our prescribed combat air patrol area. After an uneventful two hours going round and round, we were relieved by six P-38s, and as I turned to head back to Guadalcanal with my seven Corsairs, the Lightnings climbed right up past us. Within a minute they were jumped by a number of Zeros. There was no warning – we never had them on radar and they weren't reported by coast-watchers. They probably flew well to the south of the Solomons' cloud cover and came in for a surprise attack. I heard radio chat and realised the problem immediately. Looking over my left shoulder, I was surprised to see that the P-38s had formed a defensive Lufbery circle. I put my flight on alert and I told them to prepare for combat, which involved checking that their guns were armed and main fuel tank switched on until expended. Later we would switch to reserve, thus allowing us enough fuel to return to Guadalcanal.

'The Zeros and P-38s were in a wild melée by the time we arrived, and therefore didn't see our approach. We proceeded to climb up into the battle, and suddenly a Zero dived right across my bow. For a split second I couldn't help but marvel at the beauty of the configuration of the plane – it was clean and polished, a truly beautiful looking bird. But we were out for a kill so I lined up for a full deflection shot. I tried to get enough lead and was well within range, but it wasn't enough. My wingman, Lt Raymond, who was on the inside of the turn, fired at the same time as me as he did have the lead and he duly straddled the Zero with a burst of .50 cals – it went down burning. Raymond continued to stick right with me as I came in at a second Zero that was above us at 12 o'clock. He didn't see me and I hit him – he also went down burning.

Ken Walsh seen in one of his 'No 13s' on 1 September 1943. F4U-1 BuNo 02189 was his favourite aircraft, but it was written off by a VMF-213 pilot before his second tour. If his own aircraft was unserviceable he would take whichever aeroplane was available. Although this particular F4U has 'Captain' painted on the starboard undercarriage door, Walsh at that time was still a 1st Lieutenant. He was promoted to Captain the same day he was awarded the Medal of Honor – 8 February, 1944. The aircraft is also adorned with false gun ports, a practice carried out by VMF-124's armourers in an attempt to convince the enemy that the aircraft was more heavily armed than it actually was! Some of VMF-213's aircraft were similarly painted, as that unit used -124's ground-crews for a time (*USMC*)

'We began operations from Munda on the evening of 14 August. The following day, after my third combat for the 15th, I was sent to remain on station with five Corsairs covering the invasion of Vella Lavella. We were to prevent dive-bombers coming in and hitting our troops on the beach. I got on station and I was soon warned by the fighter director aboard one of the supporting destroyers – "Red 1. We have a bogey coming from the north west – it's a large bogey". I replied, "Roger. Request advise Munda to scramble what they can". I was low on oxygen so I couldn't reach high

altitude where I would have preferred to have been, so I vectored my second section leader, Capt Wally Sigler (5.333 kills), to go up to high altitude instead. He was to be the top cover while I stayed down low with my wingman. Then the Zeros came in with some *Vals* and I got underneath the latter, shooting down two before a Zero clobbered me. He got on my tail and hit me with cannon shells, one of the rounds exploding in my starboard wing tank – fortunately the wing didn't blow off.

'Taking evasive action to escape the Zero shooting at me, I "split-S'ed" into a hard right turn, doing a 360° roll. During the manoeuvre I flew into cloud and suffered an attack of vertigo. We didn't have non-tumbling gyro horizon instruments in those days, so I had to try and bring the Corsair back to level flight using the turn and bank indicator. I was spinning around doing 400-500 kts, and as I came out of the cloud I realised that I was commencing an outside loop, inverted, going down at 45°. I barely missed the rim of an extinct volcano, and with one aileron gone, I just managed to roll the aeroplane back into level flight. I made it back to Munda, but they couldn't repair the Corsair so it had to be scrapped and used for spares. One of the 20 mm shells had entered the wing, severed all the hydraulic lines and hit the main spar, rendering it beyond repair – we couldn't change wings due to our poor field conditions. Although outnumbered six to one on this sortie, we thwarted the attack as the remaining *Vals* aborted the mission.

'By late August we had returned to Guadalcanal. By then there were eight squadrons of Corsairs out there, not to mention additional USAAF P-38s and P-40s, and we were beginning to make a good show of both offensive and defensive operations. On 30 August VMF-124 performed a bomber escort, but as we left Russell Island (our refuelling point) my super-

Armourers reload an F4U-1 with .50 cal ammunition following a raid on the Japanese airfield at Munda Point, Guadalcanal, in June 1943. The aircraft was equipped with six Colt-Browning M2 machine guns, with 400 rounds for the four inboard guns and 375 for the two outboard weapons, making for a total of 2350 rounds (*USMC*)

This was the aircraft that Ken Walsh was flying on 15 August 1943, seen here consigned to Munda's 'junkyard' having been damaged beyond repair by enemy fire. VMF-124 pooled their aircraft when operating from Munda and Vella Lavella, and as such '114' would have been a pool aircraft that may have previously been assigned an aircraft number by a different unit (*Walsh Collection*)

A close up of the damage sustained by '114'. One of the 20 mm cannon shells entered the upper surface of the starboard wing, exploding inside the fuel tank with shrapnel exiting the wing undersurface and leading edge. Ken was surprised that it held together, and that he was able to make it back to Munda (*Walsh Collection*)

Wreckage of an A6M Zero and a Corsair scattered next to the runway at Munda. VMF-124 was based here from 14 August, and participated in the invasion of Vella Lavella. At that time the unit was commanded by Maj William A Millington, who remained the CO until March 1945 (*Walsh Collection*)

charger malfunctioned. Leaving the flight, I headed for Munda, where I was given a replacement F4U-1 by VMF-215. I took off and headed for Kahili alone. When I found the B-24s they were were being attacked by some 50 Zeros in th target area, and we soon lost one which crashed with no survivors. I dove into the Zeros and got a couple of them at high altitude. During the long fight I heard a distress call from some of the B-24s that were then near Baga Island, having departed Kahili at low altitude. I tangled with two Zeros in the target area before I was attacked and shot up. There were four of them, and they soon had me boxed in and began shooting the hell out of me. I tried to get down low to escape, and if I'd had enough altitude I would have baled out. I finally shook them off by getting down to wave top height and heading for Munda, but the engine had been hit so I couldn't make landfall. I rode it in and crashed off Vella Lavella, from where a Higgins boat was despatched to fish me out the sea.

'My flight usually comprised 1st Lts Johnston and Raymond, and SSgt Shelton. Johnston was my wingman in the thickest battles, and he was always there when I needed him. I ran up the higher score naturally, being a division leader – leaders usually had the highest scores because they got the first shot. Johnston was shot down on 1 April, having been set on fire by a Zero. He bailed out and I saw him going down, although I didn't know immediately who it was. He landed in the water and returned to base the next day. He was very angry as he got sunburnt swimming on his back for three miles. He flew with me from then on and was a great wingman. I owe my life to him as he saved me on a couple of occasions.

'On one escort mission on 12 August he came in and flicked a Zero right off my tail. He had to put my plane in his gun sight to get the lead, which was uncomfortable for him. The Zero had already put seven 20 mm and 37 0.7 mm rounds into me, and another split second and it would have been curtains. The aircraft was on fire and the cockpit was full of smoke. I said out loud, "Please God, not here", knowing that I would have certainly been captured by the Japanese if I had gone down in that area. As I was preparing to bail out, I pulled back the canopy whilst travelling at 300-400 kts and there was a great rush of air. The smoke cleared and the fire blew out, so I pulled up under a B-24 for protection and flew back to the emergency strip at Segi, New Georgia. The Corsair was badly shot up, but I managed to blow the gear down and land. I wasn't able to control it though, and the aircraft piled into the line, taking another F4U-1 with it.'

1st Lt Howard Finn also made ace with VMF-124 at this time;

'The first aircraft I shot down was a *Betty* bomber on 10 June 1943. It was a fluke, with me being in the right place at the right time. One of our troopships had been torpedoed during the night and she could only make two or three knots. The coastwatcher informed us that they had

F4U-1 Corsair 'No 4' *My Bonnie* of VMF-124 throws up a spray of water from Munda's runway in August 1943 following a tropical storm. Although neither Finn nor Walsh can recall any of their unit's aircraft being adorned with names, VMF-124 did utilise some of VMF-213's F4Us, and vice versa. As such, this may have been a former VMF-213 aircraft. This machine again has two false gun ports on each wing (*National Archives via Pete Mersky*)

VMF-124's 'D Flight' ('No 5 Flight') consisted of 1st Lt Howard J Finn (6 kills) standing at left, 1st Lt Mervin L Taylor (1.5 victories), flight leader Capt William E Crowe (7 kills) and 1st Lt Tom R Mutz, who claimed three victories. Finn was on the 14 February mission when the unit first saw combat. He chased a lone Zero and was immediately jumped by more enemy fighters. For protection he positioned himself below one of the B-24s he was supposed to be protecting – 'Some big hero!', as he said recently when interviewed for this volume (*Finn collection*)

seen three bombers on the ocean side of Choiseul, and we were directed to go out 100 miles, orbit and wait for them. We were completing the first orbit when I saw three specks in the distance. I rocked my wings to get Capt Earl Crowe's (7 kills) attention, and I pointed and he saw them too. I got one and the other members of my flight the other two. It was a satisfying sortie as we had stopped the enemy attacking the ship, which was quickly towed into Tulagi harbour to offload its precious cargo.

'My second kill was almost embarrassing – you feel bad about doing something this way. There was a big Japanese raid on Guadalcanal on 16 June, and nearly everybody launched to try and intercept the raid. We were nearing the end of our CAP when Earl Crowe, Tom Mutz and I were ordered to orbit the Tulagi Harbour area. Crowe spotted enemy aircraft and radioed "Bogies low on the water". The reply from our director was "Go get them", so we dived down to the water and took after a couple of Zeros. I slid in behind one and shot him down, then moved over to a *Val* whose rear gunner was shooting at me – I downed him too. The dive-bomber was very slow, being a fixed-gear type, so I just sat behind it with my far superior weapons and fired at will – they didn't stand a chance. In training we were taught they were "little Oriental bastards" and that kind of stuff, but I still had respect for them as pilots.

'When we first got there the Japanese had some good quality pilots. They could handle those Zeros, pulling really tight turns. Even a *Val* tried to pull a turn on me once, but he was too low and I shot him down as I could turn inside him. The ones we encountered in February 1943 were highly skilled, but their attrition was taking its toll and the skill of the pilots became considerably less as time went on. You could tell by the type of manoeuvres they would make. They would loop and roll when we first arrived, they were so confident. They were good pilots and they knew it. By the time I left in October, however, the quality had deteriorated. I would guess they had lost many good pilots, and that was to be the trend for the rest of the war.'

13

MORE F4Us ARRIVE

Marine fighter units converted to the F4U as aeroplanes became available. New squadrons arrived from the US, whilst the veteran F4F units took charge of their aircraft in-theatre. Following VMF-124 came -213, -121, -112, -221, -122 and -214. Finally, with the conversion of VMF-123 in early July, all the Solomons-based units were now equipped with the Corsair. During countless air battles all these units would amass scores against the Japanese, producing many aces in the process. VMF-213, commanded by Maj Britt, had arrived at Espiritu Santo on 2 March equipped with Wildcats. They were soon to re-equip with the F4U, however, before entering combat. Capt James N Cupp was to become the unit's third highest-scoring ace with 12.5 kills during his three tours in the Solomons. Here, he describes some of his experiences.

'Being given the chance to fly Chance Vought's new aeroplane was one thing, whilst actually physically doing so was quite another. There was only one squadron of Corsairs already on Guadalcanal, and there were absolutely no spare parts nearer than the United States. Therefore, the three planes we were given to check out in were quickly grounded as they all badly needed replacement parts. We had come down south armed to the teeth with spare parts for our Grumman F4Fs, but even before we had time to unload them they were no longer of any use to us – the Corsair even used a different starter cartridge. Lts Hartsock and Kuhn from VMF-124 came down from Guadalcanal to give us all the information they could about flying the Corsair in combat, and with their encouragement, added to the midnight oil burned studying handbooks, we soon thought ourselves competent to sit behind the controls of the beast.

'When we were all successfully checked our base CO sent the squadron to New Caledonia to collect a shipment of new Corsairs. We found them aboard the small carrier that had brought them from the US, but not one of them had been made ready to fly after the trip. When we finally got the planes to Tontouta Field in New Caledonia, our troubles really started. We were hampered by the fact that none of the mechanics knew about the new plane. After a week we gave up and started for home, with only six of the 28 planes we had taken from the carrier. Within two hours after we got off the transport at Espiritu, we were back on it again headed for Guadalcanal to relieve VMF-124. Our six new planes had to be left behind and so did our men, who were really sorry to see us go off without them. They were as anxious as we were to get into combat.

'We landed on Guadalcanal 1 April and were to operate from "Fighter Strip No 1", which was to one side of Henderson Field. When we relieved VMF-124 we took over

F4U-1 of VMF-213 catapults from USS *Copahee* on 29 March 1943. Capt James Cupp relates this novel experience in the following quote: 'When we got to New Caledonia we found our Corsairs aboard the small carrier that had brought them from the US – not one of them had been made ready to fly after the trip. Moreover, we had to be catapulted, this being a rather experimental process as we had no information as to the performance of the plane under such conditions. They had no head rests (as most Navy planes do), so the first day was spent getting the ship's carpenter to make us a wooden head rest for each plane. All of us except one made it off – a lone Corsair suffered engine failure and plunged off the bow of the ship' (*National Archives*)

their aeroplanes, and although they were now old, their men were well acquainted with them and could keep them in a dependable condition for us. We had 14 of these veteran F4U-1s to use, and if we got eight of them off the ground at once, we were extremely lucky.

'Our first job was to learn the geography of the Solomons off by heart, a process that involved becoming familiar with each island in the group individually. This was necessary in order to evade Japanese concentrations in case of a forced

landing, and to know which way to go to avoid possible patrols once we were on the ground. At that time, all of the islands to the north and west of us were dominated by the Japanese. There were, however, only a few troops to each island, and these were usually dug in along the coast. "The Slot" is the strip of open water stretching between the islands of the Solomons group from Guadalcanal to Bougainville. It is approximately 350 miles long and about 70 miles wide. Along the southern edge of "The Slot" lies Guadalcanal, with Henderson Field, together with its adjoining protective fighter strips. Next were the Russell Islands, a small group 70 miles from Henderson where additional strips were built.; then the New Georgia group (home of Munda airstrip), including Rendova Island. Kolombangara, with Vella Bomber Field., was next in line, followed by Vella Lavella, the Shortlands and then Bougainville. On the northern side of "The Slot" is Tulagi Harbour in the Florida Group; San Cristobal with Rakata Bay, and Choiseul (which extends almost to Bougainville) which only had ground troops on it. Bougainville's point of interest was the main Jap airstrip of Kahili, whilst the bay just off the strip was the loading point for shipping headed down "The Slot". Balale was a small island in that bay, and boasted a busy little fighter strip.

'The tactics that Maj Britt had been drilling into us for months were essentially the same as for other fighter squadrons. Each unit, however, had its own particular way of interpreting those tactics. This difference was usually in the air discipline, and the control the leaders had over the men flying with them. VMF-213 had trained as one unit longer than other squadrons operating in the Solomons, and because of this we enjoyed the reputable distinction of sticking together in combat. The fact that we all got along so well added a great deal to our value as a squadron. Two pilots flying together must know each other by heart, and know what to expect of the other fellow in any given situation. The wingman, flying blind on his leader, must trust him implicitly when they fly a tight formation or

Capt Cupp standing on the wing of F4U-1 'No 7' *DAPHNE C*, BuNo 02350. He claimed his first two victories in this aircraft (a *Betty* and a Zero) on 15 July 1943. Although three whole kills are visible, his next claims amounted to 2.5 Zeros on the 17th whilst flying BuNo 02580. The remnants of a 'No 13' are located beneath the canopy, this having been one of Ken Walsh's aircraft during his first tour *(Cupp Collection)*

This rare aerial view of an F4U-1 on a combat mission in April or May 1943 was taken by USAAF B-24 gunner Bob Lundy of the 424th Bomb Squadron, 307th Bomb Group. The aircraft has a white 'No 13' and two kill marks, together with a three-word name on the cowling. Although not known for certain, this could be a picture of an aircraft flown by Cupp or Walsh *(Cupp Collection)*

Jim Cupp, wearing his standard Solomons outfit, stands on the propeller hub of F4U-1 'No 7' *DAPHNE C* – the aircraft was named for his wife Daphne Cupp. The remnants of a 'No 13' can again be seen, this time located on the centre forward area of the cowling. This aircraft later wore four kill marks following his victories on 17 July, even though these were scored in F4U-1 BuNo 02580 (*Cupp Collection*)

Jim Cupp sitting on the nose of F4U-1 'No 15' *DAPHNE C,* BuNo 03829, in which he gained his fifth and sixth victories on 11 September (a *Tony* and a Zero). The next day he strafed Kahili in this Corsair, destroying ten aircraft on the ground, plus two barges. Cupp was credited with 12 aerial victories before being shot down whilst attempting to claim his 13th victim whilst flying F4U-1 BuNo 03803 (*Cupp Collection*)

when they are coming home at night through stormy weather. The leader is the only one flying on instruments, the only one that knows just where the next mountain is and just when the field will pop into view. The wingman must trust his leader more than he trusts himself. If he waivers in his decision to follow his leader into what seems to him to be a hopeless situation and goes off on his own, he will be lost sooner or later. At the very least he would be of no use to the squadron as a whole. By the same token, the leader must know what he is doing at all times, without exception.

'Our squadron of 30 men was divided into three flights of eight pilots, with the extra pilots being split over each flight. The flights were broken down into two divisions of four planes. Due to the nature of our assignments, and the scarcity of planes, usually only a division was designated for a complete mission. Once in a while, however the whole flight would go together. Later, when more planes were available and missions were more involved, three divisions were usually the order of the day, although we never sent up more than 16 Corsairs – when we had that many planes, we didn't have enough pilots! The division was flown in a stepped down formation. The leader's wingman was below, back and to his right. The second section of two planes were farther back, down and to the leader's left. Directions were passed by visual signals. When a flight was involved in a mission, the two divisions would stay in the same sky and if any direction had to be given, they were transmitted over the radio.

'Air discipline was most important during bomber escorts. There were many assignments to be had while covering a bomber formation, both above and below. The closer your assigned position was to the formation, the more immovable you became. Often fighters were assigned as forward guns for the bombers, and were stationed in close above and below the formation. While there, your job was to fire only on attacking planes approaching the formation head on. The others were to be left strictly alone. Neither could you follow an enemy plane after an attack to finish him off or see if he would burn or crash – your job was to stay put. With a plane as capable as ours, it was almost an impossible task. The divisions covering the formation 1000 to 2000 ft above us were not much better off either. They could attack incoming planes from any direction, but couldn't press home their advantage after the attackers had pulled off. If a pilot should succumb to ambition and pull away from his colleagues to go after one of the enemy, he would most likely find himself in amongst a

1st Lt Foy R 'Poncho' Garison on the wing of F4U-1 'No 20'. He shot down two Zeros on 30 June 1943. 'On 17 July Gregg Weissenberger's division started back from a raid on Kahili. "Poncho" was flying the No 4 position. A formation of Zeros started tagging along out of range, but he could not resist the temptation. He peeled off and attacked them. Before anyone in the division knew he was gone, he was on his back in flames.' This was how Jim Cupp described 'Poncho's' demise (*Cupp Collection*)

swarm of them in a very short time.

'The plane I was assigned was a smooth running job. With constant care on the part of my mechanics, it was ready for almost every assigned mission. It only had one drawback – the engine had never been overhauled, and by then I had some 300 hours on it. Usually a Navy plane is taken to the "cleaners" every 60 hours, but this one had been in constant service since its combat debut. So it was that at sustained slow speeds the carburettor would invariably flood out and stop the engine. Each morning during the period in question we were assigned missions to Munda escorting slow flying Dauntless dive-bombers. We never ran into any aerial opposition on these excursions, but the thing that wore me down was that temperamental plane of mine. The speed of the bombers was 120 kts and we were throttled back as far as we could to stay with them. It took just about two hours for my carburettor to flood out, and it took two hours to get right on top of the enemy airfield. Every morning at exactly the same spot, for two straight weeks my engine quit cold. A few thousand feet and a few minutes would elapse before I could get it cleared out, started, and warmed up enough to get back home. Ted (my wingman) would stay with me all the time and knew what was going on. As for the others, they always contended that I was tired of flying formation and wanted a little better view of the damage the bombs were doing.

'On 25 April Maj Peyton took his division to Munda to do a little strafing and stir things up in general. On the way home, he found himself some 10,000 ft below a sizeable force of enemy fighters and bombers. He nosed over to one side and started to climb up at them. Unfortunately they saw our four planes before they had sufficient height and started to attack. The second section had dropped behind in the attempt to gain altitude, and received the brunt of the first assault. Lt Eckart went down first, never to be heard of again, whilst Lt Peck managed to knock down one of the aggressors before receiving a burst in his engine that sent him limping home. Major Peyton and Lt Vedder (6 kills) continued weaving defensively trying to gain altitude until the latter was hit and had to set down – he returned days later with only a small shrapnel hole in his thigh. Maj Peyton came home with 82 holes in his F4U and a scratch on his wrist. They got seven of the Zeros and the bombers turned back.

'On 11 May we greeted VMF-124 as they came in to relieve us, and we had a party that night in celebration. From somewhere the mess officer drew out some steaks for the few of us left by 12 o'clock. Afterwards, every last one of us was sick – we had been living too long on *Spam*, crackers and K-rations for so long we just couldn't take "real" food any more.'

Following six weeks of R&R in Sydney, Australia, VMF-213 returned to Guadalcanal for their second tour. Capt Cupp continues:

'We knew that the campaign for Rendova and Munda was to start soon

F4U-1 'No 11' *Defabe*, seen at Guadalcanal, was flown by 1st Lt George C 'Yogi' Defabio. He claimed a Zero on 30 June and two more on 11 and 17 July 1943. 'We operated from Munda and Guadalcanal, shuttling back and forth between the two bases in ten- to fourteen-day stretches. As Munda had been our object of destruction for so long, it seemed strange to call it "home". Defabio had almost ended his days there a few weeks before. During a strafing mission an AA burst clipped 46 inches off his wing. He was practically out of the plane before he realised it would still fly if he kept up enough speed – somehow he was able to make it back to the "Canal"' – Jim Cupp (*Cupp Collection*)

and our prime ambition was to get in on it. In the meantime, our mechanics had replaced the men of VMF-124 and so, when we relieved their pilots, we were a complete outfit once more. We spent the first two weeks getting all the planes into shape for the gruelling action ahead. More F4U-1s had been added to our flight logs since we left and only a few of the old ones remained. To add to this total, factory-fresh Corsairs were being ferried up from New Caledonia, and before long each one of us had his own individual plane and mechanic. One of our enlisted men, Don Buhrmann, gave our aircraft the individual names and designs that we had so long dreamed about. Gus had a gopher painted on his fuselage, Poncho had a fierce looking eagle and Treffer, having a plane that was always out with some mechanical difficulty, had a reluctant dragon painted on his machine.

'The daily "milk-run" to Munda had completely neutralised the airstrip there and also at Kolombangara, ten miles across the channel. Thus, when the Marines landed at Rendova the opposing airpower had to come down from Kahili. The American plan was to set up a force on Rendova and later cross over to Munda. Our job was to keep a constant patrol over the area to repel anything the Japs sent down. Difficulties arose from the distances involved. Operating from the "Canal", we were 200 miles from our patrol station. It was no easy trick to shuttle back and forth on the hour-and-a-half trip and still keep fresh planes on station at all times. Each patrol would take over four hours from take-off till landing and, as we were short handed in our unit, most of us flew three patrols a day.

'Although constantly in the air, I was never able to contact enemy planes. Action always took place just while we were landing or taking off, or else we were kept out because of the screen of cumulus clouds that always hung over the islands. Soon we were the only division who had not made contact and this gave concern to Maj Gregory Weissenberger (5 kills). He wanted every pilot in the squadron to have his share of victories, but without any individual playing the hero and getting more than everybody else. After the training we had, it was mostly a proposition of being in the right place at the right time to get your bag of planes. The pilot with the high score might look good in the papers back home, but his score was likely to cause dissension among his fellow pilots, and it would become difficult to practice the teamwork necessary for an effective fighting unit.

'Our torpedo planes and dive-bomber crews have never been properly credited for the role they played. In every encounter they would go straight into the target and let the enemy try and knock them down with anti-aircraft fire. When it came to an aerial attack their slow and clumsy planes didn't stand a chance against enemy fighters. On 17 July we escorted a group of these boys to Kahili to get some troopships that were attempting to reinforce the depleted garrison at Munda. There were only three in my division that day – Ted, Sgt. Hodde and myself. This made mutual protection more difficult than with a full division of four planes.

Another 'wet strip' shot taken at Munda on 26 August 1943. 'When operating from Munda the Japanese made a determined effort to see that our forces got no farther. By then the might of Kahili was pretty well exhausted, but new enemy airfields had sprung up all over Bougainville, with reinforcements coming down from Rabaul. As Munda was subjected to shuttle bombing each night (thus, living conditions were not too good), it was thought that 14 days was a long enough dose for a fighter pilot who had to fly all day' – Jim Cupp (*National Archives via Pete Mersky*)

'A Corsair below us soon got into trouble with a Zero astern. We steepened our dive and came up behind him. Ted and I both opened up at the same time and he burst into flames. We veered away from the exploding plane and became separated. I started out to the rendezvous area just south of the Shortlands. I appeared to be the only fighter in the area so when I saw some TBFs and SBDs being molested by Zeros I turned back to fight. Three of the enemy planes, seeing a lone Corsair, decided to take care of me. It was dog-eat-dog and I was the bait. I soon found, however, that as one would get on my tail within firing range, I could roll fast to the right and come in a "split S" manoeuvre. Invariably the Zero would pull up and stall instead of following me. It happened time after time and, if I was fast enough coming around, I could pull up behind him while he was stalled and give him a burst before the next guy got on my tail. Knowing my F4U was faster, they probably thought I was diving for home, and that it was useless to try to catch me. They never did catch on and soon there were eight Japs playing "ring around a rosy" with me. I soon thought better of tackling them single-handed and high tailed it home.

'The rest of the boys had left long ago, but I soon ran into some bombers that had been hit and were limping home. When I caught up with them they were playing cat and mouse with two Zeros that had chased them out of Kahili, going in and out of the clouds trying to avoid their assailants. One of the Zeros had just finished a pass from the rear as a bomber entered a small cloud. He pulled straight up the side of the

1st Lt Wilbur J 'Gus' Thomas standing by his F4U-1 'No 10', *GUS'S GOPHER*. He became VMF-213's leading ace with 18.5 kills. His first four kills and a probable were claimed on one mission on 30 June 1943. Thomas was a well-liked and respected pilot who was unfortunately killed in a flying accident on 28 January 1947 (*Cupp Collection*)

19

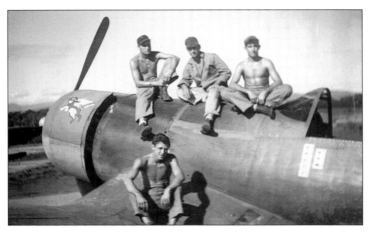

Groundcrew posing on *GUS'S GOPHER* showing the *Disney* character nose art on the port side. Eight kills are displayed beneath the canopy, although he had reached only seven victories and one probable by 15 July – he then shot down a further three Zeros on 11 September. Thomas claimed 16.5 victories with VMF-213 in the Solomons, and was then further credited with two more Zeros on 16 February 1945 whilst the unit was aboard USS *Essex* (*Cupp Collection*)

cloud to avoid over-running the bomber inside and it was a simple matter for me to catch him as he topped the cumulus – he went back down the other side in flames. His partner had nestled under the cloud to catch the bomber as it came out, and when he saw his friend fall, he turned around and went back to Kahili. I stayed with the bombers until they were back in friendly territory, and then headed home.

'After each flight, we reported to Lt Harrison, the intelligence officer attached to us, and gave him the particulars of the flight. He assembled all the combined information, but it was often difficult to get the right story from a bunch of excited pilots as our reports usually seemed like a mass of unconnected events. For example, the following action details an average mission.

'30 June 1943 – My division, Lts Brown, Votaw, Spoede and myself scrambled at 1115, and were ordered to Rendova to intercept a flight of about 30 Jap planes. We climbed to 25,000, from 1215 to 1300 but saw no enemy planes. Rendova was pretty well closed in, but we could observe the landing operations progressing without interruption. We landed at Guadalcanal early that afternoon and stood by our planes and waited. At 1350 word was received that VMF-221 and VF-11 had made contact with the enemy. At 1545 my four planes, along with Lt Sheldon Hall's division, comprising the latter (6 kills), Shaw (14.5 kills), Morgan (8.5 kills) and Jones, were scrambled and told to cover the shipping off Rendova. Hall's division was about three minutes behind mine on the take-off. The radar wasn't working well so we were told to keep our eyes open. We climbed to 15,000 ft, reporting on station at 1645. A stranger was reported at 8000 ft, coming in on the shipping. We dived to attack, but could find no enemy planes. It was cloudy and all the action that we could hear on the radio was taking place behind some clouds, so we never got a glimpse of it. At this time Rendova reported nine floatplanes to the west, but we were again unable to make contact. After searching the sky for half an hour, we continued the patrol until we returned to base at 1915.

'Maj Weissenberger, Capt Cloake and Lts Thomas (18.5 kills), Drake, Defabio, Garison, McCleary and Boag were kept on scramble alert, while we were on our first flight. They took off just as we landed and were ordered to proceed to Rendova. The Major's flight was airborne at 1400 and they arrived over Rendova at 26,000 ft at 1445. Lt "Yogi" Defabio was late. He took off at 1405 and proceeded in the hope of joining up on the Major, but was never able to locate him. However, after circling the area over Rendova, he heard over the R/T a "Tally-Ho" call signalling that the fight was on. Defabio dropped to 8000 ft, where he saw two Zeros and made a run on the leader from the Zero's left and above. He fired, causing him to smoke, burst into flames and dive into the water below. He saw many other Zeros and attempted to attack them, but could find none that were not already engaged by friendly planes. When the fight was over he was joined by Lt Garison, and they returned to base.

'Maj Weissenberger and Lts Thomas and Garison attacked a group of about 15 to 20 Zeros that they had sighted below. The Major shot down three Zeros before being shot down himself. After shooting down his first two Zeros, he met his third coming at him head on. Both fired point blank. The Zero burst into flames and exploded, while the Major's plane began to smoke and

caught fire. He was able to bail out at about 800 ft, and his parachute opened just before he hit the water. Luckily, he landed near a US destroyer that picked him up and returned him to Guadalcanal. He received only minor injuries consisting primarily of painfully bruised ribs, the result of hitting the tail of the plane when he bailed out.

'Our workload was by now comparatively light. We only flew two patrols a day, instead of the usual three. As we were so low on pilots, other squadrons were borrowing our excess planes, thus helping us to get out of more work. The invasion of Munda was now a certainty. The Japs were coming down the slot with increasing regularity. We lost two more planes before our tour was up. It happened when we were heading off a bunch of Jap dive-bombers. We came upon them late and had to go under their formation to get at the ones that had already peeled off. Their attack was stymied, but we left ourselves open to the rear. One of Ted's adversaries took full advantage of the situation and filled his fuselage full of lead. By 26 July, Doc Livinggood had grounded us all because of fatigue.'

After another trip to Sydney the unit received new personnel in preparation for their next tour. Maj Weissenberger was replaced at this junction with a new CO, Maj J R Anderson. Capt Cupp continues the story:

'When operating from Munda our beautifully marked planes were put into a pool and assigned to different pilots from different squadrons every morning. That alone was enough to break our hearts, but when the SEEBEEs (who had been pressed into service as mechanics) asked us where to inject the gas and oil we were almost tempted to draw our pay and go home. There were a few bona-fide mechanics on the strip, but they had always worked on Grummans so our sleek little planes went without much maintenance. They rapidly became dirty and undependable. They always kept going, but little things were always cropping up to

Maj Gregory J Weissenberger straps into his F4U-1 Corsair 'No 9', BuNo 02288. He took command of the unit following the death of Maj Wade H Britt, Jr, who was killed when his aircraft ran off the runway, hit another two Corsairs and exploded during an early morning take-off (*USMC*)

A fine view of Maj Weissenberger's aircraft as the engine roars to life, with the crewchief standing by with a fire extinguisher in case of an emergency. The tape on the gun ports was used to keep dirt from entering the barrels during taxying and take-off. The cowl flaps were always employed on the ground to prevent the engine overheating (*USMC*)

Maj Weissenberger takes off from Guadalcanal's 'Fighter One' strip in June 1943. He became an ace on 18 July 1943 by shooting down a Zero – his fifth and final victory. The Major celebrated his new ace status with a 'birthday cake' later that afternoon (*USMC*)

F4U-1 Corsair 'No 5' of VMF-213 has its guns boresighted using an apparatus constructed out of coconut logs. Boresighting was a frequent topic of conversation among Corsair pilots, as the procedure needed to be carried out regularly because the guns moved slightly in their mounts each time they were fired. The distance at which the .50s were boresighted varied from unit to unit, the usual distance being around 900 feet (*USMC*)

annoy you. Some would conk out when you changed blowers. Some would run rough all the time; keeping you in suspense as to whether or not it would get you back.

'The Marines were getting ready for another objective in their stepping stone campaign up the Solomons. This time it was to be Bougainville itself and it was up to the air arm to soften up Kahili and Ballale in the same way we had with Munda. To increase our airpower, the SEEBEEs were building another fighter strip at Vella Lavella (about 40 miles up the chain). The Jap bomber strip at Kolombangara (about ten miles across the bay from Munda) was no longer in use. AA batteries would still fire on us though if we got too close. There were one or two floatplanes up one of the streams close to that strip, but they could never be located in daytime. At night they would harass the troops behind us and once in a while, aid in keeping us awake by dropping a stick of bombs on Munda. It only added to the nuisance of the shuttle-bombers ("washing-machine Charlie") which operated all night long.

'Walley was on my wing now, with Avery and Stewart flying the second section. They hadn't seen any aerial combat yet and were anxious for the inactivity to stop. We were on our way to patrol over Vella Lavella on 17 September when the news came in that a large formation of bogies was headed our way – their initiation was about to occur.

'The sky was dotted with white clouds that stretched up to 18,000 ft. We started to climb towards the southern tip of the island dodging the clouds all the way. We nosed through a hole and saw a massive formation of dive-bombers ploughing in about five miles away from us and at the same height. At hat instant I looked up and saw a string of eight Zeros zigzagging across the sky, less than 100 ft above my head. We turned over on our backs and headed for cover, whilst we radioed the Jap position and course. The Zeros saw fit not to accompany us, so after a few thousand feet we hauled up to try it again. The second section lost a little ground in the manoeuvre. We headed along a parallel course to the bombers, looking for another hole in the overcast to poke through. By that time there was quite some distance between our two sections. It was not long before we saw an opening and headed through it. This time the Zeros were looking straight down their guns at us as we repeated the operation, and this time they

F4U-1 'No 8' *Eight Ball*/*Dangerous Dan*. Although this aircraft was later pictured with one kill marking under the canopy on the port side, it is uncertain as to exactly which pilot gained the victory in this machine (*USMC*)

attacked. The mistake they made, however, was to get in between our two sections. As we all headed for a lower altitude, Avery and Stewart were behind them merrily blasting away. They soon reduced the odds to "even Steven" and the remaining Zeros left my tail.

'In the meantime, the bombers were approaching their target. By the time we again regained our altitude, we found most of them already in their dives and there were only a few left at our height. They were old and slow planes and it was difficult to stay behind them long enough to get in a good burst before we passed over them. We came up from behind, cut our engines and just sat there. We could almost reach out and touch them as our six guns opened up. The one I was on looked like a toy suddenly thrown to the floor. Pieces started flying off and suddenly there was nothing there. In the distance, I saw one already in his dive and for some reason, I determined to get him if I never did anything else. At first, all that was possible was to follow him down and avoid the AA as much as possible. I was glad to notice that Stewart was with me. We levelled off just above the water and I moved over to him. I had been so focused on the one plane that I was surprised to discover another bomber flying alongside of him, and then another and then another. I looked up and discovered the whole area covered with them. We had followed my prey to the rendezvous point where all the planes assembled in formation for their return to Kahili. Their only defence was a light calibre machine gun handled by the gunner in the rear cockpit.

'I pulled back the throttle to keep from over-running them. It was almost pathetic to witness their futile efforts to evade destruction. They were already less than ten feet off the water; and all they could do was skid from side to side. I came across one with a very strong desire to live. He threw his plane around with all his might and it was hard to keep my bullets going into him. First the gunner slumped over and next the engine started to blaze. In an instant, the whole thing was one flaming torch skidding over the water. I pulled up and crossed over the top of Stewart and came down again. The plane ahead of me jerked around violently and I closed without firing. The nearer I got, the more violent were his evasive manoeuvres, until finally one wing hit the water and he crashed. Without having fired a shot, I pulled up crossed back over Stewart and continued up the line. I was disheartened to find that their gas tanks were bullet proofed, but we did well in spite of it. Everytime I looked back over our course I saw a plane hit the water. I was able to count three of Stewart's, though it was difficult to keep track of him. Four of mine hit the water, but it was impossible to watch the effect on most of them.

'We were nearing the head of the column, just finishing off one

F4U-1 'No 4' of VMF-213 undergoes maintenance in the open at Guadalcanal in June 1943. The tape on the gun ports appears to indicate that this aircraft was equipped with ten wing guns! Even though VMF-124's ground echelon was replaced by that of VMF-213 in early June, the practice of indicating false gun ports was continued by both units (*USMC*)

together, when my little world began to fall apart. A 20 mm shell came through the tail and exploded the CO_2 bottle behind my seat. The noise scared me out of my wits. Another came over my head and hit the accessory section just behind the engine and a third knocked a hole in my left wing, carrying my flap away. There were four Zeros above and behind me getting ready to take turns at me. Stewart had pulled ahead and didn't respond to my radio call – undaunted, I pressed the send button, hurriedly giving my position, adding the earnest cry "Help!" I was sure I couldn't stay in the air long. I would have set the plane down right there, but I was sure my opponents wouldn't have been content just to see my plane go in. The alternative was to shove the throttle forward and pray – I did both. My beautiful, faithful, greyhound of a plane responded like a bat out of hell. They must have been surprised, for they just sat there and watched me go. I was away in no time. When I left, they turned their attention to Stewart. He was also able to outrun them, but not before his plane became hard to handle from all the extra lead he was carrying. He climbed for altitude and bailed out. He came home the next day after an eight-hour ride in a native war canoe.

'My division was not assigned a flight on the 19th so we volunteered for the dawn patrol the next day. "Charlie" came over on the hour all that night and, as we took off at 0500, I could see his silhouette 10,000 ft. above. Making a quick join up, we started after him. The boys came in close in order to see my wings in the darkness. I kept my eyes glued to the hazy blur in the distance that was the Jap *Betty*. We knew we had a long chase ahead of us; he was speeding away and we would have a long climb to get up to him. We were almost over the mountain of Kolombangara before it became apparent that we were gaining on him.

'The plane I had grabbed checked out fine on the ground, but as we got over the water the fuel pressure gauge started wavering – the normal pressure was 15 lbs per square inch., but the needle was at eight and still going down. I checked over the gas supply and turned on the electric fuel pump, but to no avail. I called the division and told them I might have to turn back. I asked them if they were able to locate the bomber. They spread out a little in order to divert their attention to the sky ahead, but couldn't see the enemy aircraft. I couldn't disappoint them while there was still a chance as we were on the same level as "Charlie" now, and about a 1000 ft behind. Our aim was to get above and ahead of him before starting our attack, but as my needle was still going down, I wobbled my wings and started in from where we were. I wanted to pass the 13 mark on my score!

'I dived underneath him, thinking that I could make one pass on his unprotected belly and then return to base. The boys would pick him up as I passed him. My intention was to attack straight up and miss the cannon in his tail that could only fire down at an angle of 45°. The impression still remains in my mind that, as I came up, the bomb bay opened and a gun started firing down from that unorthodox position. I was hit three times before I could wink an eye. All three hits seemed to centre around the bottom of my cockpit. When I looked down, there was a small flicker of flame starting to take hold. All the experience of months of combat seemed to surge up inside me, and before I could think I had my radio disconnected, the safety belt and shoulder straps unfastened and the hood of my canopy thrown back. It was when I stood up in the seat and attempted to climb over the side that thought returned. My plane was pushing through the air at more than 300 kts and the stream over my cockpit was like a steel wall holding me in. I could not get out!

'The air whipping into the cockpit had fanned the spark into a blow-torch that swept up my legs as I sat back in the seat. The throttle arms next to my left leg were still on full, but I could not make that hand move to pull it back. I brought my left arm over to my right and hooked onto it. I watched as my right arm was dragged through the flames and deposited on the throttled which I slammed closed. I tried to get out again, but again was forced back. One thought mounted until it excluded all others – "How simple it would be just to ride her in." At that time the pain stopped in my legs and the mental turmoil subsided. Complete satisfaction and contentment engulfed me. It seems the feeling was with me for hours to account for the vivid picture it left me, but I know it was actually over in a split-second. I had been straining for freedom with my legs braced against the rudder bars and then the tail was coming at me. I raised my legs to clear the elevators and then I was on my own – the plane was gone.

'I remembered my parachute and wondered if it was still on me. I found that it was and pulled the ripcord. I didn't feel it open, but I noticed the risers braced against my back attached to something solid above. Almost at once I saw the plane crash into the water below. The sock on my left leg was still smouldering and I began to feel it. Reaching down I snuffed it out with my good hand. The rest of my clothes had not caught fire – I suppose they didn't have time. My legs were covered with a white ash that used to be skin, but they didn't hurt much at that moment. My face and right arm had not been burned so badly and the surface nerves were still working. My hair was all gone and pieces of skin hung around my lips. I hurt like the devil!'

Capt Cupp's squadron-mates managed to down his intended victim while he was picked up around 1430. Badly burned, Cupp was hospitalised for 18 months, undergoing 14 operations. His final combat tally was 12 1/2 officially credited kills.

Armourers adjust the three port-side wing guns of F4U-1 *Bubbles* to facilitate boresighting at Guadalcanal. This appears to be a VMF-213 aircraft, but again may well have also been used by VMF-124 too (*USMC*)

25

Colour Plates

This 18-page section profiles many of the aircraft flown by the elite pilots of the US Navy, US Marine Corps and the Fleet Air Arm. Also included are notable machines that are representative of the Corsair's all-important, but often ignored, ground attack mission. All the artworks have been specially commissioned for this volume, and profile artists John Weal and Mark Styling, plus figure artist Mike Chappell, have gone to great pains to illustrate the aircraft, and their pilots, as accurately as possible following much in-depth research. Aces' machines that have never previously been illustrated are featured alongside acccurate renditions of the more famous Corsairs from World War 2.

1
F4U-1 black 17 of 1st Lt Howard J Finn, VMF-124, Guadalcanal, February 1943

2
F4U-1 white 13/BuNo 02350 of 2nd Lt Kenneth A Walsh, VMF-124, Munda, August 1943

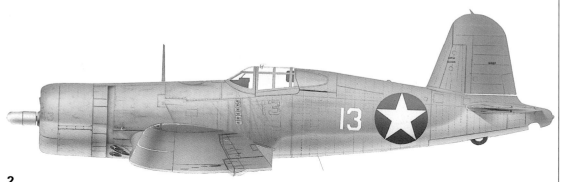

3
F4U-1 white 114 of 2nd Lt Kenneth A Walsh, VMF-124, Munda, August 1943

4
F4U-1 white 13 of 1st Lt Kenneth A Walsh, VMF-124, Russell Islands, September 1943

5
F4U-1 white 7 *DAPHNE C*/BuNo 02350 of Capt James N Cupp, VMF-213, Guadalcanal, July 1943

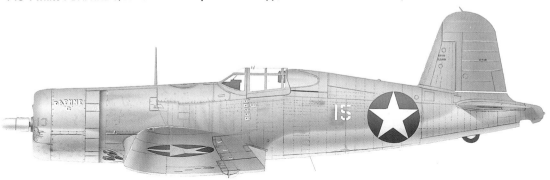

6
F4U-1 white 15 *DAPHNE C*/BuNo 03829 of Capt James N Cupp, VMF-213, Munda, September 1943

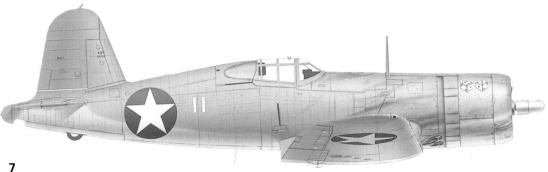

7
F4U-1 white 11 *Defabe* of 1st Lt George C Defabio, VMF-213, Guadalcanal, July 1943

8
F4U-1 white 10 *GUS'S GOPHER* of 1st Lt Wilbur J Thomas, VMF-213, Guadalcanal, July 1943

9
F4U-1 white 10 *GUS'S GOPHER* of 1st Lt Wilbur J Thomas, VMF-213, Guadalcanal, July 1943

10
F4U-1 white 20 of 1st Lt Foy R Garison, VMF-213, Guadalcanal, July 1943

11
F4U-1 white 125/BuNo 02487 of 2nd Lt Donald L Balch, VMF-221, Guadalcanal, July 1943

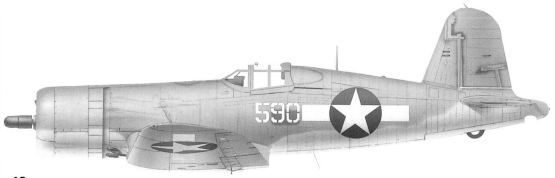

12
F4U-1 white 590/BuNo 17590 of Capt Arthur R Conant, VMF-215 Barakoma/Torokina, January 1944

13
F4U-1A white 735/BuNo 17735 of Capt Arthur R Conant, VMF-215 Barakoma/Torokina, January 1944

14
F4U-1 white 75 of Maj Robert G Owens, Jr, VMF-215, Munda, August 1943

15
F4U-1 white 76 *Spirit of '76*/BuNo 02714 of Maj Robert G Owens, Jr, VMF-215 Munda, August 1943

16
F4U-1A white 596/BuNo 17596 of 1st Lt Robert M Hanson, VMF-215, Torokina, February 1944

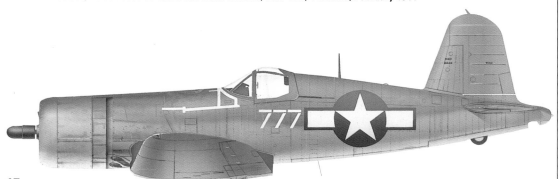

17
F4U-1A white 777/BuNo 17777 of 1st Lt Phillip C DeLong, VMF-212, Vella Lavella, November 1943

18
F4U-1A white 722A/BuNo 17722 of 1st Lt Phillip C DeLong, VMF–212, Vella Lavella, November 1943

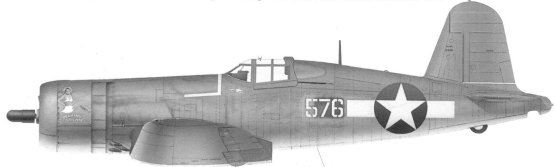

19
F4U-1 white 576 *MARINE'S DREAM*/BuNo 02576 of 1st Lt Edwin L Olander, VMF-214, Munda, October 1943

20
F4U-1 white 93/BuNo 17430 of Capt Edwin L Olander, VMF-214, Vella Lavella/Torokina, January 1944

21
F4U-1A white 740/BuNo 17740 of Maj Gregory Boyington, CO of VMF-214, Vella Lavella, December 1943

22
F4U-1A white 883/BuNo 17883 of Maj Gregory Boyington, CO of VMF-214, Vella Lavella, December 1943

23
F4U-1A white 86 *Lulubelle*/BuNo 18086 of Maj Gregory Boyington, CO of VMF-214, Vella Lavella, December 1943

24
FG-1A white 271/BuNo 13271 of Maj Julius W Ireland, VMF-211, Bougainville, January 1944

25
F4U-1 white 17-F-13 of Lt(jg) James A Halford, VF-17, USS *Bunker Hill*, August 1943

26
F4U-1A white 1 *BIG HOG*/BuNo 17649 of Lt Cdr John T Blackburn, CO VF-17, Ondonga, November 1943

27
F4U-1A white 19 of Lt Paul Cordray, VF-17, Ondonga, November 1943

28
F4U-1A white 15 of Lt(jg) Daniel G Cunningham, VF-17, Ondonga, February 1944

29
F4U-1A white 9 *LONESOME POLECAT* of Lt Merl W Davenport, VF-17, Ondonga, January 1944

30
F4U-1A white 34 *L.A. CITY LIMITS*/BuNo 17932 of Lt(jg) Doris C Freeman, VF-17, Ondonga, November 1943

31
F4U-1A white 29 of Lt(jg) Ira C Kepford, VF-17, Bougainville, January 1944

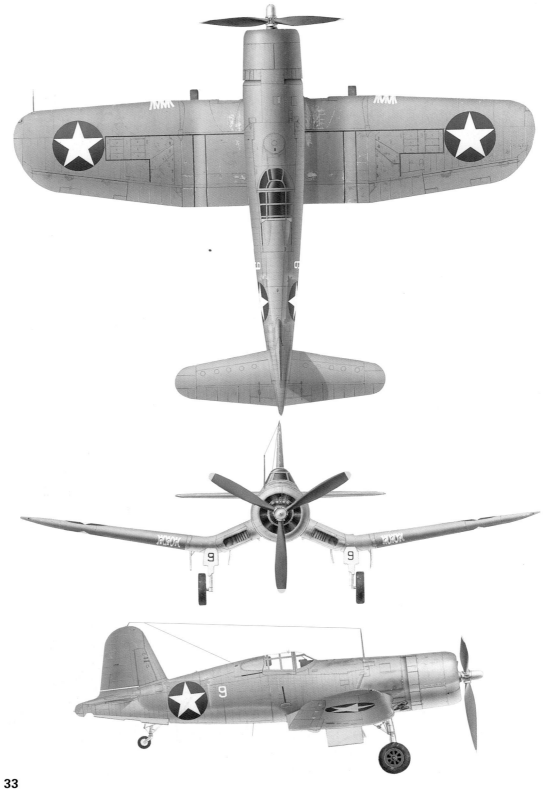

33
F4U-1 white 9/BuNo 02288 of Maj Gregory J Weissenberger, CO of VMF-213, Guadalcanal, June 1943

32
F4U-1A white 29 of Lt(jg) Ira C Kepford, VF-17, Bougainville, January 1944

34
F4U-1A white 17/BuNo 18005 of Lt Cdr Roger R Hedrick, VF-17, Bougainville, March 1944

35
F4U-1A white 25 of Lt Harry A March, Jr, VF-17, Bougainville, May 1944

36
F4U-1A white 8 of Lt(jg) Earl May, VF-17, Bougainville, January 1944

37
F4U-1A white 22 of Ens John M Smith, VF-17, Bougainville, February 1944

38
F4U-1A white 3 of Ens Frederick J Streig, VF-17, February 1944

39
F4U–1A white 5/BuNo 17656 of Lt(jg) Thomas Killefer, VF-17, Bougainville, February 1944

40
F4U-2 black 212 *Midnite Cocktail* of Capt Howard W Bollman, VMF(N)-532, Kagman Field, Saipan, April 1944

41
FG-1A yellow 056 *Mary*/BuNo 14056 of Capt Francis E Pierce, Jr, VMF-121, Peleliu, November 1944

42
F4U-1A white 108 of Maj George L Hollowell, VMF-111, Guadalcanal November 1943

43
F4U-1A black 77/NZ5277, RNZAF, Solomons, 1945

44
F4U-1A white 122 of VMF–111, Gilbert Islands, 1944

45
Corsair II white TRH/JT427 of Maj Ronald C Hay, RM, No 47 Wg, HMS *Victorious*, January 1945

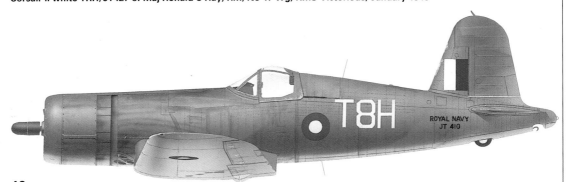

46
Corsair II white T8H/JT410 of Sub Lt Donald J Sheppard, RCNVR, No 1836 Sqn, HMS *Victorious*, January 1945

47
F4U-1D white 1 of Maj Herman H Hansen, Jr, VMF-112, USS *Bennington*, February 1945

48
F4U-1D white 167/BuNo 57803 of Lt Cdr Roger R Hedrick, VF-84, USS *Bunker Hill*, February 1945

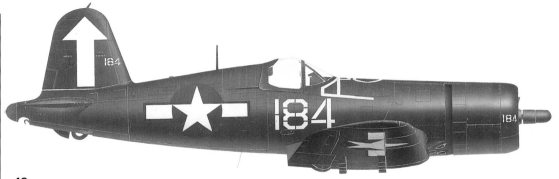

49
F4U-1D white 184 of Lt Willis G Laney, VF-84, USS *Bunker Hill,* February 1945

50
F4U-1D white 66 of Ens Alfred Lerch, VF-10, USS *Intrepid,* April 1945

51
F4U-1D yellow FF-59 of Lt Col Donald K Yost, CO of VMF-351, USS *Cape Gloucester,* July 1945

52
F4U-1D white 6 of Lt Joe D Robbins, VF-85, USS *Shangri-La,* December 1944

53
F4U-1C white 11 of Lt Joe D Robbins, VF-85, USS *Shangri-La*, May 1945

54
F4U-1D white 51 of 1st Lt Robert Wade, VMF-323, Okinawa, May 1945

55
F4U-1D white 48/BuNo 57413 of 1st Lt Jack Broering, VMF-323, Espiritu Santo, October 1944 to March 1945

56
F4U-1D white 31 of 1st Lt Francis A Terrill, VMF-323, Okinawa, May 1945

57
F4U-1D white 26 of 1st Lt Jerimaiah J O'Keefe, VMF-323, Okinawa, April 1945

58
F4U-1D white 207 of 2nd Lt Marvin S Bristow, VMF-224, Okinawa, May 1945

59
F4U-4 white 13/BuNo 80879 of Capt Kenneth A Walsh, VMF–222, Okinawa, June 1945

60
F4U-1D white F-107 of 1st Lt Phillip C DeLong, VMF-913, MCAS Cherry Point, North Carolina 1944

1
Capt Arthur R 'Rog' Conant of VMF-215 at Torokina in January 1944

2
Capt Harold L Spears, also of VMF-215, at Bougainville in December 1943

3
Maj Gregory 'Pappy' Boyington at Vella Lavella in December 1943

4
VMF-214's 1st Lt John F Bolt, Jr, at
Vella Lavella in early 1944

5
Maj Ronnie Hay, RM, aboard HMS
Victorious with No 47 FW in 1945

6
Lt Harry A March, Jr, of VF-17 at
Bougainville in May 1944

TOROKINA AND MUNDA

VMF-215 arrived at Espiritu Santo in July 1943. Under the command of Capt J L Neefus, they began their first combat tour by attacking Japanese bases in the northern Solomons. They moved to Munda on 12 August to complete their first tour, with their second spell in the frontline beginning in October under the command of Lt Col H H Williamson. Based at Vella Lavella from 28 November, they soon began attacks against heavily defended airfields on Rabaul. Maj Robert G Owens (7 kills) was given command of the unit on 6 December, and duly led it throughout its third tour, much of which was flown from Torokina – the unit occupied the island strip on 27 January 1944. This squadron was one of the few Marine Corsair units to keep virtually the same personnel throughout its long combat career – other squadrons would rotate back to the US, and when they returned to combat would be staffed by new pilots, thus making them in effect completely different units. During the war VMF-215 accounted for the destruction of 135.5 enemy aircraft, and produced ten aces, one of whom, Lt Robert M Hanson, was posthumously awarded the Congressional Medal of Honor.

Maj Bob Owens and his wingman, Capt Roger Conant, had served with the squadron right from the start of its combat career, and they both became aces – Owens claimed seven whilst Conant accounted for six. Here, they describe some of VMF-215's operations.

Conant – 'Our original aeroplanes at Santa Barbara had the early birdcage canopy. As soon as we had enough F4U-1s we loaded them aboard ship – a seaplane tender – and sailed to Hawaii. There we lost three pilots as they were so hot to get into combat that they volunteered to go up to the front straight away. However, they went to the mid-Pacific and never saw combat at all!'

Owens – 'The aeroplanes we flew in combat were sadly not those we brought over from the US. When it came time for us to go down to the Solomons, we got our orders and packed our bags. Just then, another unit arrived at Midway to relieve us – VMF-212. We went aboard the ship and they went ashore, swapping aeroplanes in the process. I was really reluctant about that. Compared to those of other units, we thought our Corsairs were the best maintained. Here we were about to go into combat and we had to give up our F4U-1s and take those of

F4U-1 Corsairs of VMF-215 fly in formation off Hawaii in early 1943. 'We flew our aircraft from Barbers Point, Hawaii, to Midway. The Corsair was almost unique in that it had wing tip tanks located inside the wing. These tanks contained 50 gallons of fuel, which we used for long flights. We would use the fuel and then open up the vents and purge the air with CO_2 so that you didn't have a combustible mixture left in them. We thought this a much better arrangement than carrying drop tanks. Midway was a great place, and being isolated there was nobody to bother you. Whilst on the island we did three months of training, which in the long run saved our lives. We had had no flight time on the Corsair until then' – Capt Roger Conant (*Conant Collection*)

F4U-1 'No 76' *Spirit of '76*, BuNo
02714, being pulled from the mud at
Munda on 14 August 1943. Although
this aircraft has been reported to be
Bob Owen's machine, he only ever
flew it once in combat, on 31 July
1943. His wingman, Roger Conant,
also flew this machine on 1 and 4
August, and so did Ed Olander of
VMF-214 on 13 October 1943. None
of these pilots gained victories in it,
however (*National Archives*)

It would appear that Bob Owens
did, however, use this machine –
F4U-1 'No 75' – quite frequently,
however. Although VMF-215 pilots
did not have aircraft assigned to
them, Bob Owens flew another F4U-
1 – BuNo 17927 – on 13 consecutive
missions, during one of which he
gained two victories on 14 January
1944. He also flew another F4U-1 –
BuNo 02656 – on 12 different
missions, during which he gained
one victory and a probable on 21
and 12 August 1943, respectively
(*National Archives*)

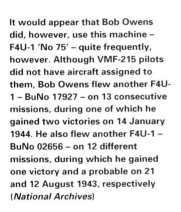

VMF-212 in return. We didn't even know if their groundcrew knew how to turn a bolt correctly!

'When we went into Munda it was the first time (since Guadalcanal) that there was a group of squadrons flying similar machines. Each aeroplane had a number on the side from 1 to 16. Having been assigned to fly a mission in "No 5", I'd get out there on the line and there would be five "No 5s" – five squadrons each with a "No 5"! So we repainted the aircraft with numbers that weren't like those of other units, most squadrons tending to use the last three digits of the BuNo. From then on you were told by the engineers "You take 'No 672' and you take 'No 345'. Every time it was different, and my log-book shows that I rarely flew the same aeroplane twice. We also used other squadron's F4Us. When Maj Hugh Elwood (5.1 kills) commanded VMF-212, we had an agreement to share our aeroplanes. We decided that one day he'd take them and we'd have them the next. We'd take whatever planes were available and put our pilots in them. We pooled the aircraft because we always had more pilots than we had Corsairs. There was a time when our aircraft were painted with personalised markings. Various pilots in our unit made suggestions and the aircraft were duly painted up. I authorised the painting of an aircraft with the legend *Spirit of '76*. Contrary to what has previously been suggested, I only flew that aircraft once. Like the other pilots, I took whatever machine was assigned for any given mission.

'The Corsair was a hell of a thing to fly, particularly if you'd started on a much lighter aircraft. It had so much torque that when you "poured the coals" to 2800 rpm, it would try to walk away from you. You had to have full rudder on there in order to keep control. The F4U had a very large cockpit, so much so that the shorter guys could not hold their rudder all the way in to counteract the torque. Some pilots used to fly with a cushion – one of my pilots, Lt Hap Langstaff, used to have two of them in there in order to be able to push the rudder pedals further forward.

'We were based at Munda, New Georgia, for three or four weeks and I

don't remember ever seeing my bed during the daytime. When we were flying in and out of there, the ground forces were still fighting. During that time Lt W D Demming was shot down in a very unusual way. As he was coming around in to land he was hit by an enemy artillery shell. They aimed at him purposely, and I heard they painted an American flag on the side of the gun! He managed to bail out of the plane but ruined his arm and was evacuated to the US. We never heard from him again.

'On 15 August 1943 we were covering the Marines landing at Vella Lavella. We were way up at altitude and up through the clouds came four Zeros. We went down after them, and as much as I'd been trying to instill into everybody (including myself) "don't shoot until you get right up on them", I started firing about a quarter of a mile away. By the time I got up close to them I'd expended my ammo and I didn't hit a soul.'

Conant – 'One of our most important tasks was bomber escort. On a typical mission we would have 50 to 70 planes stacked at three different levels – low medium and high cover. The medium cover would sometimes fly very close to the bombers, at the same level or just below them. Our divisions were made up of two pairs which would continuously weave back and forth. As a result, we always had somebody facing outwards ready for an attack. If we had spare F4Us available after a number of our aircraft had been assigned for a mission, we would also send up an extra division that we called "Roving Cover". These pilots could go anywhere they chose and could attack the enemy ahead of our formation.

'At the beginning (when I only had around 250 hours of flight time) the only thing I knew how to do was fly wing. So I'm flying wing on Bob and I'm only ten feet away. He's out shooting at planes, and the only thing I saw all day was him! We decided that I wasn't doing either of us any good just sitting on his wing so we loosened up a little bit – when he'd turn, I'd cut inside, etc. We made a mission up to Kahili escorting B-24s, weaving back and forth. After hitting the target they flew into the clouds. Once you fly into clouds, you don't get any more cover. We were free to go. Bob takes off; shooting at Zeros with me following behind him. The thing was, he was shooting and other people were tailing in on him. So when they got behind him, I'd be right behind them. I shot two of them off his tail at that time, one of which was a *Tony* (Kawasaki Ki 61).'

Owens – 'Once, we followed a B-24 down close to the water that had been shot up over Rabaul. There were two Zeros down there, and they were being flown in true fashion, being able to turn on a dime. There was also a Corsair tucked in close to the B-24. We came down from altitude making pretty good speed. I got behind one of them and followed him. He just pulled right up and kept going. I kept going after him shooting, but I never hit him. When he got to the top of his climb, we both ran out of everything. At that point I was out of speed and all

Conant claimed six kills with VMF-215 flying as Bob Owens' wingman, before going on to lead his own section. On 30 August 1943 he was on ground alert at Munda with his F4U when Ken Walsh appeared and 'stole' it. Walsh's F4U-1 (BuNo 02585) had a supercharger problem, so he landed at Munda and Capt Neefus, CO of VMF-215 gave him permission to take a readied F4U as a replacement (*Conant Collection*)

Conant destroyed a Zero on 14 January 1944 whilst flying F4U-1 'No 590', BuNo 17590, during a mission to Rabaul escorting SBDs and TBFs. Conant began the mission at Barakoma, then flew to Torokina to refuel before heading to Rabaul. The F4U was photographed whilst undergoing maintenance at Vella Lavella on 10 December 1943 (*via Jim Sullivan*)

I was worried about was staying alive. He stalled I guess, and came back down. As he passed by me he was only 50 ft away, and I could see his guns flashing. There I was out of everything, and all I was trying to do was get that F4U flying again. I didn't hit him at all, so I wasn't the world's greatest shot after all!'

Conant – 'At that point Bob decided it was time to get up in the clouds. We both headed up and Bob made it. I'm going up hanging on the prop, just about to make it in, and there's a Zero over on the left. He's shooting like mad. "Shit, I ain't gonna' make it with this guy shooting at me." I just pushed it straight over and I got away too. Air combat is not a highly disciplined affair.'

Owens – 'On one mission we ended up being credited with half a plane destroyed. VF-17 was involved I think. We were escorting a B-25 flight from New Guinea on a mission to Rabaul. It got off to a bad start as we were not warned that the bombers were coming. For intelligence we had what we called "Indian Talkers". Because everybody was breaking everybody else's code, we got these guys from some tribe to come over from the US. We would have Indians on each of the islands. They would radio information back and forth by "Indian Talk". You almost couldn't break it as there was no rhyme or reason to what they said. The Indians screwed up that day and the B-25s appeared right over us, unannounced. They made one turn over Torokina and headed off to the target without escort. We were manning planes like crazy to try to catch up with them.

'We passed them coming back after they'd hit their target. The weather was not all that good. We broke out into what I call an amphitheatre, as you could see everything within a big clear area. I only saw three Japanese planes. I was shooting at one of these three and another plane came right down in between us. Finally, I said to myself "If you want to stay alive, you better get the hell out of here". We had 40+ aeroplanes trying to shoot these three little Japanese machines. I pulled off to the side and I saw two of them go down into the water and crash. The third little guy, from my perspective, actually got shot at by all 40+ aircraft. He finally went right down to just above the water. All of a sudden he hit the water and just blew up. Later, there were about ten people arguing over who shot him down. So somebody decided that we would get half the credit and so would the other unit.'

Conant – 'Although I was on the same 18 January 1944 mission as Bob, and it sounds like the same incident in which I was involved, it

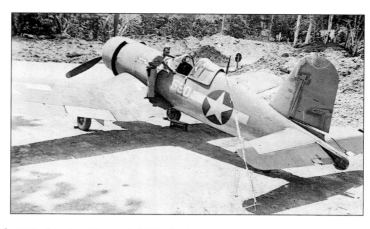

Another view of F4U-1 'No 590', this time at Munda. It appears to be wearing a field-applied three-tone scheme, together with field-applied white bars on the national insignia. The machine lacks the curved glazed area directly aft of the canopy which was standard to most of the early 'bird cage' canopy-equipped aircraft. It is also fitted with the shorter aerial mast located aft of the cockpit, rather than the tall forward-mounted type associated with early production aircraft (*via Jim Sullivan*)

Roger Conant destroyed another Zero on 18 January 1944 whilst flying this machine, F4U-1A 'No 735', BuNo 17735. The aircraft was pictured at Bougainville during February painted in a very stained three-tone scheme, with field-modified national insignia (*National Archives*)

isn't. Smitty, Jake Knight and I were a threesome that day, and the B-25s were coming out just as we were going in. We caught these three planes and they were going the other way. I'd shoot at one and he'd take off in one direction with either Smitty or Jake going after him. I'd shoot at another one and he'd go off in another direction and the other pilot would finish him off. I shot the third one and hit him good. I hit him right in the cockpit – blew the

VMF-215 personnel pictured at Vella Lavella. Bob Owens, at centre, was at that time recuperating after being shot down by his own wingman on 24 January 1944. Although initially given credit for the kill, Roger Conant (front, far left of picture) was not responsible for Bob's unplanned swim in Simpson Harbour, Rabaul (*Conant Collection*)

hell out of him. He circled around and I stayed with him. I pulled up alongside of him and we were only 50 ft above the water. My last vision of him was of his arms up protecting his face, with flames coming out of his engine. I didn't see him go in. This sounds so similar but it isn't because there were only three of us shooting at these planes. The interesting thing about this combat was the calibre of the Japanese pilots encountered. We had caught three of them. Only six months earlier three good pilots would have gotten' away, and they would have been shooting back at us, but we got all three of them. Furthermore, as we pulled out of this thing and all reformed, when we looked up, there were *five* Zeros all sitting in a little column above us. They had obviously seen us, and they must have seen the other guys go in. They were above us while we were low, slow and out of ammunition. They had us dead to rights, but we just turned around, got into a wild scissors and flew out. They never bothered us.'

Owens – 'I was shot down on 24 January, but there's no mention of it in my log-book whatsoever. Roger Conant flew wing with me for a long while. When he quit flying wing he commanded a second section. One mission, when we were heading up to attack Rabaul, I had a kid flying wing – he was a really young guy. This was his first combat mission. The new guys coming out were 18 or 19 and we had to take care of them. I called them kids because I was an old man of 24! As was our custom, if there was a new guy in the outfit we'd let him fly out front. This was because the guys at the back would get hit harder if we were attacked. We were flying on a real economical power setting so that we would save all

VMF-215 pilots pose next to a derelict Nakajima Ki 43 *Oscar*. This was the JAAF's most widely used fighter, and would appear to have been commonly mistaken for the Navy's Zero by Allied airmen judging by the official loss records of both Japanese services. Like most enemy aircraft, the *Oscar* was highly manoeuvrable, but it was lightly armed and lacked armour protection – unless flown by an experienced pilot, it was easy prey for the Corsair (*Conant Collection*)

our fuel for when we got there. We were observing radio silence, but after a while this young boy finally said in a meek voice, "Skipper. Could you throttle back a little? I can't keep up". I knew who it was, and I looked over in his direction. I knew he was nervous and I motioned to him and throttled back.

'The way our attacks worked, we'd escort TBM Avengers or SBD Dauntlesses and they'd be down below us. They would go in low and we would do a big circle around

them as they dived down. That particular day the Zeros were up there. The *Vals* were rolling over and peeling off to attack the ships anchored in the harbour. As we were going down, believe it or not, this kid passed me about three times. By this time I'm running wide open, and I've got the throttle pushed forward all the way to the firewall. I was really going and he couldn't stay behind me, when before he hadn't been able to keep up!

'Coming off the target, our tactic was to get around behind the bombers. Most of our planes would get in this position to cover any lagging planes; that's where the danger was. I pulled up, making a wide circle around so I would be behind the last guy. Lo and behold, right in front of me was a type of plane that I'd never seen before. Later I found out it was called a *Tony*, but at that time I thought it was a Bf 109. I was going much faster than this aeroplane – he was trying to get in behind the stragglers. I pulled in behind him, but I guess I screwed around a little more than what I should have, only managing to get in a short burst. He was turning, I was turning, and when I hit him again the wing came off at the root. I flipped as hard as I could to get away. Instead of just going down, the lift from just one wing flipped him up and over the same way. I had to change my direction in a hurry from going one way to getting the hell over the other way. Suddenly, there was a hell of a commotion and I was on fire. I was still a little way over the harbour at Rabaul. I got down to the water and all the guys threw their dye-markers on me. A PBY picked me up in 30 minutes. The word got out that my wingman had shot me down, which I'm sure he did. He'd been behind me and was shooting at the same guy. I know he didn't intend to do it as I flew right into where he was shooting, but he shouldn't have been shoot-

ing! I'm 99 per cent sure that's what happened, but I didn't ever say anything as it would have caused a lot of problems. They all thought it was Conant.'

Conant – 'The word went down to Headquarters that Bob's wingman had shot him down. The guy down at Headquarters had been with the squadron and knew that I was his wingman. So I got credit for shooting him down. The first *Tony* that *I* ever saw was when Bob was leading a division up the "Canal". One flew right in front of us. We were so surprised he was gone before we ever knew it. He probably never even saw us.'

Three of VMF-215's high scoring aces pictured together at Bougainville in early 1944. From left to right, 1st Lt Robert M Hanson (25 victories and 2 probables – two of his kills took place when he was with VMF-214), Capt Donald N Aldrich (20 victories and 6 probables) and Capt Harold L Spears (15 victories and 3 probables) (*USMC via Pete Mersky*)

1st Lt Hanson poses next to his battle-damaged F4U. This official USMC photograph is dated 4 August 1943, and claims the Japanese opponent responsible for the 20 mm cannon hits was a Zero which Hanson then shot down. On that date he scored his first victory, and his opponent was in fact a *Tony* – Hanson was then serving with VMF-214 (*USMC via Pete Mersky*)

THE 'BLACK SHEEP' SQUADRON

VMF-214 first made the transition to Corsairs in June 1943, whilst commanded by Maj H A Ellis. The squadron was to become famous under the command of Maj Gregory 'Pappy' Boyington (28 kills, 22 in F4Us). The 'Black Sheep' produced nine aces, among them the then 1st Lt (later Captain) Edwin Lawrence Olander. He gained five victories and four probables flying the Corsair during two tours with VMF-214, and recounts his varied combat experiences in the following interview.

'I was a "civilian soldier" – I began training as a naval aviator a few months prior to Pearl Harbor and returned to civilian life at the end of 1945. My military experiences were happy and exciting ones, but I never harboured a desire or intention to make the military a career. My flight training was primarily at Pensacola, after which I was assigned instructor's duty at Jacksonville Naval Air Station. Flying SNJs, my instructing consisted primarily of escorting a half-dozen pilots on a course out over the Atlantic and supervising the passes they made at a towed sleeve firing live ammunition. From a position about 1000 ft above the tow plane, and considerably forward of it, they would, one by one, turn back towards the sleeve and at the appropriate time roll into a dive and fire at the banner, returning to the formation to repeat the process.

Maj Gregory Boyington, CO of VMF-214, is handed baseball caps in exchange for kill decals whilst in the cockpit of F4U-1A 'No 740' (BuNo 17740) by second-ranking 'Black Sheep' ace 1st Lt Chris Magee (9 kills). VMF-214 pilots were to receive a cap from a World Series player for every Japanese aircraft downed (*USMC*)

'Pappy' Boyington with other VMF-214 pilots. He claimed 22 victories and 4 probables with the Corsair, preceded by six claims with the AVG in China. On 3 January 1944 whilst flying an aircraft loaned to him by Marion E Carl, his squadron was engaged by Zeros of the 204th and 253rd *Kokutai* near Cape St George, New Ireland. He claimed three Zeros whilst his then wingman, Capt George M Ashmun, scored another victory. In turn, they were both shot down, with Boyington remaining a PoW for the rest of the war (*via Pete Mersky*)

F4U-1A 'No 883', BuNo 17883, was occasionally flown by Boyington, as well as by his wingman Robert W McClurg. The latter became an ace on 23 December 1943 when he destroyed two Zeros over St George Channel. He went on to claim a total of seven confirmed victories and two probables, and following his service with VMF-214 returned to the US as a fighter instructor (*National Archives*)

I would critique and rate their performance and we would discuss the results when examining the sleeve for hits back at base. Besides this target shooting we did other things such as night formation flying and a little bit of one-on-one dogfighting, a skill we never used when later tangling with Japanese Zeros – they were much too manoeuvrable for us to engage in dogfights. Because of my instructor's duties, when I shipped out to the South Pacific in the spring of 1943 I had about 600 hours in the air, versus the 200 common for many when faced with combat. With these extra hours came increased self-confidence.

'In Espiritu Santo, in the New Hebrides, I was assigned to a pool of pilots. We were there to replace other pilots lost in combat or rotated back to the USA. However, the need soon arose for another fighter squadron in the ongoing Solomon Campaign. The then Maj Gregory Boyington, who had experience with the American Volunteer Group in China, was available for command, and thus VMF-214 was reconstituted in the field at Espiritu. The "training" we did during the few weeks before we flew to the Solomons, and combat, was really a misnomer. Some of the pilots had scarcely flown the F4U and so they had checkout and familiarisation flights. Boyington went out with all of us in two or three four-plane divisions at a time so as to judge what kind of a hand he'd been dealt when the pilots were selected from the roster. Mostly he sat and talked with us, telling us what to expect in the weeks ahead. In September 1943 we headed the 548 nautical miles north to Guadalcanal to join the aerial assaults on Bougainville.

'There were 28 of us, all pilots except for an intelligence officer (Frank E Walton) and a squadron doctor (Jim Reames). We had no ancillary personnel, and no planes assigned to us – throughout our two combat-tour existence we "borrowed" the Corsairs we flew, and the services of those who cared for them. Having no planes of our own, we simply climbed into any machine made available to us and took off, Boyington included. In the Solomons all I flew was the F4U-1, the old "birdcage" model, with its restricted visibility canopy.

'After six weeks of daily combat flights over Bougainville (mostly from Munda, New Georgia) we repaired to Espiritu again to reform. When we returned to the Solomons in November our roster had increased to 40. Once again we were all pilots except for the same intelligence officer and doctor. By this time the airfields and the Japanese air power over Bougainville had become impotent. A landing on the west coast of Bougainville had resulted in a perimeter sufficiently large enough to contain an airstrip on which fighter planes could top off their gas tanks

1st Lt John F Bolt, Jr, an ace with six victories, devised a new system of ammunition belting for VMF-214. He was convinced that the standard belt loading of one incendiary and one tracer, followed by an armour-piercing, was not the most effective arrangement for destroying Japanese aircraft that lacked protective armour. Whilst at Espiritu he carried out tests firing machine guns at wrecked aircraft and oil drums filled with gasoline, proving that the armour-piercing round was unnecessary. VMF-124 later eliminated the armour-piercing, instead using five or six incendiaries to one tracer. Other squadrons soon adopted the same loading, bringing about a temporary shortage of incendiary rounds in the Pacific (*Bolt Collection*)

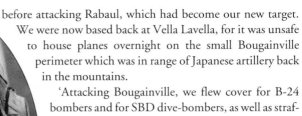

Capt Edwin L Olander claimed five confirmed victories and four probables (all Zeros) from mid-September to the end of December 1943 whilst with VMF-214 (*Olander Collection*)

before attacking Rabaul, which had become our new target. We were now based back at Vella Lavella, for it was unsafe to house planes overnight on the small Bougainville perimeter which was in range of Japanese artillery back in the mountains.

'Attacking Bougainville, we flew cover for B-24 bombers and for SBD dive-bombers, as well as strafing targets of opportunity. When flying cover for B-24s, which had much more range than us, they would fly to Guadalcanal and we'd rendezvous with them over our home base (Munda, New Georgia, when the target was Bougainville, or the Empress Augusta Bay strip on Bougainville when the target was Rabaul). Customarily, there would be up to six layers of fighter cover from, say, 15,000 to 26,000 ft, with specific altitude assignments for everyone, and the four-plane divisions would weave above the bomber formation all the way to target, or until intercepted by the enemy. The same description applied when the flat-bombers were B-25s.

F4U-1 'No 576' *Marine's Dream*, BuNo 02576, in which Ed Olander claimed a Zero on 17 October 1943 during a fighter sweep to Kahili. The aircraft is seen in December following an accident at Torokina. It has a field-applied three-tone paint scheme, and utilises the last three digits of the BuNo as an aircraft number. The national insignia has also been field-modified with the addition of white bars without a blue surround (*USMC*)

F4U-1 'No 93', BuNo 17430, waits at 'Scramble Alert' at Espiritu Santo, New Hebrides. Ed Olander flew a shuttle mission in this aircraft from Vella Lavella to Torokina, and from there a CAP sortie on 5 January 1944 (*National Archives via Pete Mersky*)

F4U-1A Corsair BuNo 17736 of VMF-216 following battle damage sustained on a mission to Rabaul on 10 January 1944. VMF-216 claimed 27.33 victories (all with the Corsair) mostly on missions to Rabaul (*USMC*)

Corsair pilots scramble for their aircraft at Guadalcanal in early 1943. F4U-1 'No 68' wears a field-applied three-tone scheme and field-applied bars on the national insignia. The curved glazed area aft of the early 'bird cage' canopy has been sealed on this particular machine (*via Pete Mersky*)

F4U-1s and F4U-1As of VMF-216 are lined up next to the newly completed runway on the first day of operations at Torokina Point, Bougainville, on 10 December 1943. Sea-Bees had quickly carved three strips out of the jungle following the landings at Empress Augusta Bay. The landings were hotly contested by the Japanese as part of Operation *Ro*. During a 16-day period, ending 17 November 1943, they lost 191 aircraft from units based at Rabaul, and from the remnants of their carrier air fleets (*USMC*)

'Rabaul was too distant for the SBD dive-bomber to reach, but going to Bougainville we provided them with pretty much the same staggered cover, with one crucial difference. The SBD was at its most vulnerable once it had completed its dive and dropped its bombs. It had insignificant speed and no power to regain altitude. Besides the fighter cover the SBD's only protection was a single .30 cal weapon operated by the rear-seat gunner, who literally went into combat on his back, looking up. Gawd, I felt sorry for those fellows! Our job was to weave over them all the way down and protect them as they made their way home – hard flying for all of us. VMF-214 was, of course, not the only squadron present. Usually planes from four to six Marine squadrons would be involved, as well as a couple of Navy squadrons flying F6Fs and New Zealanders flying P-40s.

F4U-1s warm up prior to a mission at Torokina Point on 10 February 1944. There was a concerted effort by the Japanese to oust the Americans from their new base, and on 8 March shells began falling on the airfield which led to the nightly evacuation of aircraft to avoid destruction. Machines from the base flew ground attack missions against the attackers, whose offensive finally ended on 24 March (*USMC*)

Marine Corps personnel relax on the beach at Torokina Point whilst an F4U-1A departs in the background. There were three airstrips at Torokina, one right next to the beach and two more inland at Piva Uncle and Piva Yoke for bombers and fighters respectively (*National Archives via Pete Mersky*)

'Most fun of all were the fighter sweeps when we flew over their airfields to "pick a fight" – i.e., engage any enemy planes which chose to come up to meet us. Often, it was wild! Except for strafing missions the fighter sweep was the only other primary function of the fighter plane. My best description of a fighter sweep is: a bully goes into a school yard with a chip on his shoulder and says "Let's fight". Boyington led us on many of these and if we met no enemy planes over their bases he'd taunt them via radio to come up and fight. They always did and it was always a wild melée which defied description. Japanese supply lines were stretched and it was harder and harder for them to replace lost planes and pilots. Our fighter sweeps were designed to hasten the attrition, and they succeeded. Our trips to Rabaul

A relieved Maj Thomas M Coles of VMF-212 with his F4U-1A, BuNo 17937, at Vella Lavella on 20 January, 1944. He successfully landed his aeroplane even though the rudder had been shot away during an air battle over Rabaul. Three days later he got his revenge by shooting down two Zeros over Duke of York Island. VMF-212 gained a total of 127.5 victories with the F4F and F4U, all bar two of which were claimed in the South West Pacific theatre (*USMC*)

1st Lt Harold E Segal of VMF-221 pictured next to his Corsair on Russell Island on 17 July 1943. At this time he had five victories, but went on to claim a further seven bringing his total to twelve. His last two victories occurred on 24 January 1944 whilst he was with VMF-211. VMF-221 were credited with 155 kills, whilst VMF-211 claimed 91.5 (*USMC via Pete Mersky*)

Capt James E Swett of VMF-221 claimed a total of 15.5 victories and was awarded the Congressional Medal of Honor. He shot down seven *Vals* during a two-hour period on 7 April 1943 whilst flying the Wildcat, and went on to claim a further 8.5 kills in the F4U (*USMC via Pete Mersky*)

Capt Donald L Balch sits beside his Corsair. He served with VMF-221 for the entire war, gaining two victories in the Solomons and another three whilst on the USS *Bunker Hill*. 'On 6 July 1943 my division was directed from the Russell Islands to New Georgia. There we were jumped by several Zeros which we broke up like a covey of quail, each division going in a different direction. I got onto the tail of one Zero and shot him down. I then started looking for the other members of my division whilst simultaneously patting myself on the back for my splendid marksmanship. All of a sudden all hell broke loose, with part of my hatch disintegrating along with some of the instruments in front of me. I immediately "split S'ed" out to the left and down, pulling out at around 6000 ft, never having seen anything. My wingman joined up with me and, because I couldn't hear anything on my radio, kept pointing at my tail. We then turned home and flew back to our base. I put my gear and flaps down on final, but I lost complete control of the aircraft on flare out. I cut the power and slammed into the runway. We found later that my controls had been badly shot up, just holding together until the moment I flared out for my landing' – Balch (*Balch Collection*)

were the same. The island was a mighty fortress, being Japan's Pearl Harbor in the South Pacific, with planes coming up to greet us from four airfields. Its loss would be a very serious blow to the Japanese, and we witnessed this in the intensity of their fighting.

'Boyington was shot down in St George Channel, near Rabaul, in early January 1944, only to reappear from a Japanese prison camp at war's end. Soon thereafter, our squadron returned to Espiritu where it was soon deactivated. The "number" was sent back to the mainland where the squadron was reformed. Along with other "Black Sheep" pilots, I was assigned to VMF-211 and we did a tour based on the Green Islands, near Rabaul. I saw no more air combat, but we continued to be shot at as we patrolled New Ireland and the northern tip of New Britain around Rabaul, but that tour was relatively unexciting.

'Returning briefly to "Pappy" Boyington, whom we squadron mates were more likely to address as "Greg", "Skipper" or "Gramps" – he answered to them all – I can

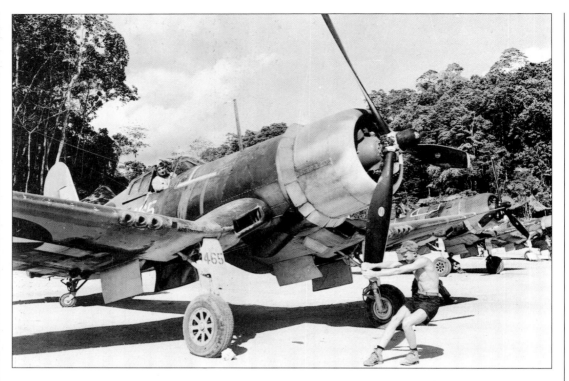

F4U-1 Corsair 'No 465' of VMF-222 has its prop 'run through' prior to flying a mission from Green Island in 1944. This unit gained 50 victories in the South West Pacific, before participating in the Philippines campaign and then moving on to Okinawa on 22 May 1945. There, it gained its last three victories of the war (*via Jim Sullivan*)

say this with conviction, that when countries are facing a crisis such as war, inevitably some men step forward and lead when leadership is most needed. Greg Boyington was such a man. He inspired those 50 of us in his VMF-214 to achieve over and above our own most optimistic expectations. He also inspired others in squadrons with whom we fought side by side. He may have been a roughneck of sorts, he may have consumed too much whisky too often and he may not have been the classic officer and a gentleman, but he loved and supported the men with whom he fought. And, on a daily basis, he provided a quality of leadership of which few others were capable. The pity is, I guess, that he was never able to reach the heights he could have. I'm grateful that I knew Greg Boyington at his best – in combat.'

F4U-1As on a mission fly high over Espiritu Santo during March 1944 (*USMC*)

US NAVY CORSAIRS

The first US Navy unit to receive the F4U was VF-12, commanded by Lt 'Jumpin' Joe' Clifton – the squadron began to receive aeroplanes in October 1942. As the pilots trained in their new aircraft serious problems emerged that were to effect the operational deployment of the F4U. Trials aboard USS *Sangamon* showed that the aircraft was, at that time, ill-suited to carrier operations. The problems largely related to its deck landing and taxying characteristics. The undercarriage legs were found to have overly stiff oleos and would require modification to eliminate the aircraft's tendency to bounce on touchdown. There was also a tendency for a wing to drop on approach, this being due to torque stall. Bad visibility from the early 'bird cage' canopy was further decreased by oil leaking from the hydraulically actuated cowl flaps. Modifications had to be quickly introduced on the Chance Vought production line to alleviate these problems.

When VF-12 finally deployed to the Pacific they gave up their F4Us in exchange for F6F Hellcats, despite having become carrier qualified on the Corsair in April 1943 aboard USS *Saratoga*. By that time the Navy was equipping all its carrier-based fighter units with the F6F, and only had logistic support for the Grumman fighter. Because

Early F4U-1 Corsairs of VF-12 on a training mission in the US in late 1942 (*via Phil Jarrett*)

of this one-type only maintenance and spares set up adopted by the fleet, the Navy decided to deploy its third Corsair squadron, VF-17 'Jolly Rogers', as a land-based unit. They duly became only the second Corsair-equipped Navy squadron operating in-theatre, following in the footsteps of Lt Cdr W J 'Gus' Widhelm's VF(N)-75, who had commenced operations with F4U-2 Corsair nightfighters from Munda on 11 September. This unit consisted of just six pilots, but all of these men had performed

F4U-1 Corsair '17-F-13' of VF-17 is seen just after a landing during the unit's Carrier Qualification cruise. The aircraft has the new three-tone scheme applied, but with the early style national insignia. It bears four kill marks, victories claimed by Lt(jg) James A Halford during his earlier service at Guadalcanal flying the F4F Wildcat. He was detached by VF-17 due to combat fatigue, gaining no further victories in the Corsair (*via Jim Sullivan*)

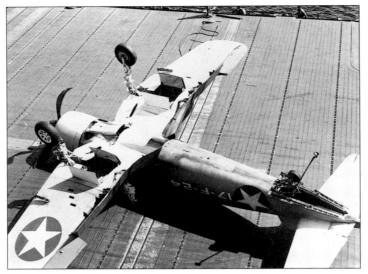

F4U-1 Corsair '17-F-24' of VF-17 on its back following a carrier landing mishap aboard USS *Bunker Hill* in August 1943. Although the early Corsairs (especially the 'bird cage' canopy version) were difficult to land on board a carrier, both VFs -12 and -17 did become carrier qualified in the type. Modifications to the oleos were made by VF-17 during their deployment to *Bunker Hill* which overcame the aircraft's tendency to bounce on touchdown. Nevertheless, neither unit went into combat with their Corsairs aboard a carrier, VF-12 exchanging their F4Us for Hellcats, whilst VF-17 deployed as a land-based squadron (*via Jim Sullivan*)

at least one prior combat tour, Widhelm, for example, having previously flown SBDs – most of his pilots had 2000 hours flying time on average. The Navy's wish to deploy VF(N)-75 in full squadron strength was scuppered by manufacturing delays in the construction of the hand-built radar sets fitted in the specially modified F4U-2s.

Suffering no such problems with their 'plain' F4U-1s, Lt Cdr Tom Blackburn's (11 kills) VF-17 arrived at Ondonga on 27 October 1943. They were soon to make a name for themselves during the Solomons Campaign, being officially credited with shooting down an incredible 154 enemy aircraft in just 79 days. Blackburn had chosen Lt Cdr Roger Hedrick (12 kills) to serve as VF-17's Executive Officer (XO) when the unit was formed in early in the year. The latter had completed flight school in 1936, and had gone on to serve with a number of frontline squadrons before joining VF-17 at its inception. Known as 'Rog' to all and sundry, Hedrick served with the unit for its entire combat career. In the following interview he describes his combat experiences in the Corsair.

'We sailed from Norfolk in September 1943 aboard the *Bunker Hill* for our shake down cruise, becoming carrier qualified in the early 'bird cage' model. The Air Group Commander and higher command were all happy with our performance. We soon received the F4U-1A model which was a great improvement over the earlier "bird cage" type with its lower seat. With all that canopy framing and sitting so low it was difficult with a 12 ft nose out in front of you to see a flag waver when coming aboard ship. While at sea we received a despatch ordering us to report to ComAirSols and become a land-based squadron. Naturally we were greatly disap-

F4U-1A Corsair 'No 1' *BIG HOG*, BuNo 17629, flown by Lt Cdr John T Blackburn, is seen at Ondonga after his fourth victory, which was scored on 11 November 1943. As well as four kill marks the aircraft also has four patched bullet holes, visible to the right of the aircraft number. These were the result of Blackburn's XO, Roger Hedrick, mistaking him for a Zero. The personnel are, from left to right, Wharton, Guttenhurst, March, Jr (5 kills), Blackburn, Dr Hermann and Cpl J M Taylor – the identities of the remaining two groundcrew remain a mystery (*via Pete Mersky*)

pointed, having worked hard with Chance Vought representatives to overcome some of the basically minor difficulties that any new plane has. Nobody told us at the time that the reason for the change was that we were the first Corsair squadron on board a ship in the fleet and had we blown some tyres or had to land on a different carrier there would be no spare parts for us as there were none in the logistics chain. The Marines had been based in the Solomons since February, so they did have logistic support for the Corsair. Our first base in the Solomons was to be Ondonga, 50 miles northeast of Guadalcanal. We later moved to Bougainville, from where we launched attacks against Rabaul.

'My first kill occurred on 1 November 1943 when we were covering the landings at Empress Augusta Bay, Bougainville. I was due to go on station at about 1300 to relieve Tommy Blackburn as top cover. Shortly after leaving Ondonga with eight planes we heard the Fighter Director at Bougainville talking about a Japanese strike coming in. We speeded up to maximum climb and just at that moment my generator went out, so I turned my radio off to conserve battery power. By the time we approached the southern end of Bougainville we were at 20,000 ft. In the distance towards Buka, where there were some Japanese airfields, I saw three tiny little dots and I knew that we didn't have anybody over there. I got up sun, towards Rabaul, and got above them. They didn't see us and I was able to make an easy high side run on them. I rocked my wings rather than notify my flight over the radio; I wasn't sure if my guns would fire. In fact, I planned to just use the four inboard guns rather than the full six; I wasn't sure if there was even enough power for those. This was our first combat and I was alone out front. I had a good look at these jokers, I saw the red meatball and knew for sure that they were the enemy. Coming down I picked out the leader. We had our guns boresighted to 900 ft – at that point the wingspan of the Zero filled the 50 mm ring of our gun sight. Knowing that their gas tanks were in the wing root I tried to hit that area. In this particular case, which was like almost all the others that followed, I pressed the trigger for two to four seconds and she went up like a torch. As soon as mine went up they all "split S'ed" and headed for the deck. We kept them away from Tommy Blackburn's flight by chasing them for a while, but that was about all we got out of it.

'One week later we were directed out to intercept a large Japanese strike – bombers escorted by 29 fighters. It was the first occasion that I experienced when our radar was effective. Again I had six planes with me flying top cover above Empress Augusta Bay. We again got above them – they were flying in three-plane sections and they hadn't spotted us. I remember thinking, "Here's when we find out how good the F4U is". Diving down on them, we passed through the formation and I was astounded to seem them break up into two Lufbery circles, a completely defensive tactic devised during World War 1 by the first truly American ace of them all, Maj Raoul Lufbery (17 kills). All they needed to do was spread out, as they had a higher rate of climb than we did, at least at low altitude. We chased them and made runs across the circles and after a couple of passes they broke up. All of them against six of us. We took on one after another, and I was involved in a series of head-on runs, making three or four individual passes. I was hitting each of them in turn, and I could see pieces of their engines coming off, about two cylinders at a time, flying by me. But

Lt Cdr Roger R Hedrick, XO of VF-17, relaxes in the cockpit of F4U-1A 'No 17' BuNo 18005. He gained nine victories with the unit (all Zeros) using three different 'No 17s'. His first three were gained on 1, 11 and 17 November 1943 in F4U-1A BuNo 17659, whilst the next three occurred on 26, 28 and 30 January 1944 in F4U-1A BuNo 55798. His last three were gained in this aircraft featured here on 18 February (*Hedrick Collection*)

Hedrick again seen with Corsair 'No 17' BuNo 18005. The 'skull and cross bones' motif on the fuselage was not actually carried on this aircraft – it was scratched onto the negative for publicity purposes! It only carried the standard motif on the cowling, similar to other aircraft in the unit (*Hedrick Collection*)

F4U-1As of VF-17 fly in close
formation. The nearest aircraft was
piloted by Lt(jg) Ira C Kepford (16
victories), 'No 8' by Lt(jg) Earl May
(8 victories) and 'No 3' by Lt(jg)
Frederick J Streig (5 victories). All of
these machines lack antenna masts,
the second two having a whip aerial
instead of a spine-mounted mast
(*Chance Vought*)

Lt Merl W 'Butch' Davenport with
his F4U-1A 'No 9' at Bougainville in
February 1944. The aircraft bears
five kill marks (only four are visible)
following Davenport's victory over a
Zero on the 5th – he had previously
been credited with a quarter share
in the destruction of a *Betty* on 6
November, followed by two
Zeros on the 21st and
another pair on 30
January 1944.
Davenport went
onto claim a
further Zero to
bring his total
number of
confirmed
victories to
6.25 (*Killefer
Collection*)

I never saw anyone of them open fire
on me. There were no fire flashes
along the wings or from the prop
area. We chased each other until
their survivors headed back towards
Rabaul and we headed back home.

'On 11 November our mission
was to cover a Task Group consisting of three carriers that was to hit
Rabaul. We put our tail hooks back
on our planes, which we had taken
off to lighten them slightly. Our job
was to fly out to the Task Group and
cover them while they launched
their own planes, which were to
strike against shipping and airfields
at Rabaul and the Simpson Harbour
area. We got up before dawn and
again we observed radio silence.
There was a certain amount of cloud
cover and we were hard pushed to even find the Task Group, although we
knew fairly well where they were. We did locate them at about 0900 and
landed aboard shortly after they'd launched their aeroplanes. VF-17 and
an F6F squadron were providing cover for the ships, and I went aboard
Essex, flagship of the Task Group Commander, with half the squadron,
whilst Tommy Blackburn went aboard our old fiend *Bunker Hill* with the
rest of the unit. At 1300 we launched again, as this was the time we
expected the Japs to attack. A very large raid that came in from Rabaul and
some of our boys did a great job by stopping their attack planes from getting through to the carriers. I was again involved in a big melée that went
on for quite some time. My wingman and I were chasing one lone Zero
that was heading back to Rabaul. This guy kept managing to escape into
a cloud, just about keeping outside of firing range, so we'd have to wait for
him to emerge – this was repeated time and again, I was primed waiting
for him to reappear. Suddenly, a plane appeared and I set myself up for a
full deflection shot. Just as I pressed the trigger, I realised I was
shooting at an F4U. I instantly released the trigger and I
couldn't see if I had had any effect on the plane at all. Then
we did a join up signal and the F4U joined up on me. I
was then looking at *BIG HOG*, F4U-1A "No 1" – my
CO's aeroplane!

'I didn't know if I'd touched him until we landed
at the field where we had to refuel before heading
down to Ondonga. Then he showed me these damn
holes in his plane. He said "You lousy shot, Roger.
When those six .50s hit me, it moved the plane side-
ways". That's all he ever said to me about it. I never
guessed that Tommy would be hiding out in the
cloud – he'd been hit by about four or five Zeros and his
windshield had fogged over. Being practically blind he'd
ducked into the cloud to wait for his canopy to clear.

'We found that about 80 Japanese aircraft were always up above us, waiting for our arrival. Every day, regular as clockwork, a fresh group would come in from Rabaul. Our bosses at ComAirSols who were responsible for the strikes going into Rabaul had to provide a certain number of fighters to protect the bombers going in. We escorted Navy dive- and torpedo-bombers, as well as USAAF B-24s and B-25s. We would provide 16 planes on a given strike, and if we had more in commission that weren't required then Tommy Blackburn and others came up with the idea to send up extra fighters to surprise the Japanese by getting above them for a change. At Rabaul they had four active airfields whilst on Bougainville we only had the one strip on the 125-mile long island. The Japanese coast-watchers would radio a warning telling the defences how many aircraft we had and when to expect us. As we approached the target we would see clouds of dust on their fields indicating that their fighters were coming up to meet us. The pattern of cover over the bombers took the form of three layers. Marine F4Us and Navy Hellcat squadrons flew below us whilst VF-17 was invariably in the top cover position – the first one the Japs had to come through. The fact that we had to be tied there when the enemy was always coming down on us got a little frustrating after a while, so we usually sent four, but on occasion two, aeroplanes to patrol outside of the main strike group, coming in low from another direction so as not to be picked up on radar. They would then climb up to as high as 35,000 ft, whilst the Japanese were usually at around 20,000 ft, although one time we paid the penalty for having this height advantage as the oil in our guns froze up – I was making some runs and nothing happened, so I had to turn the lead over to somebody else, which really annoyed me.

'I was pumping those charges as fast as I could. We were able to surprise the defenders as they were totally unsuspecting. They never bothered to look up above, being dependant on their fighter directors down below for help. I was once leading the top cover flight when we had four of our boys go on ahead. Approaching the target I looked up and two burning Zeros came down out of the clouds, almost as if they were flying in formation. Then came two more followed by yet another pair. There were just two Corsairs up there, one being flown by Ike Kepford (16 kills), and they were doing a wonderful job. We then knew that we wouldn't have to contend with quite so many of the enemy. It was a very effective tactic.

'In a January 1944 I found myself totally alone, lagging behind everybody else when we were heading back home. I encountered a Zero heading back to land at Rabaul – we weren't far off shore over Simpson Harbour. He was doing what I considered to be a victory roll and I thought "That son-of-a-bitch isn't gonna' get away with that", so I went after him and clobbered him. As usual his aircraft burst into

Lt(jg) Doris C 'Chico' Freeman with his F4U-1A 'No 34' at Ondonga in November 1943. The aircraft bears two kill marks following his victories over two Zeros on 21 November. He only claimed two further probables with the unit, but later became a 9-kill ace with VF-84 in 1945. Freeman lost his life on 11 May 1945 when USS *Bunker Hill* was struck by a *kamikaze* (*Killefer Collection*)

F4U-1A Corsair 'No 5', BuNo 17656, flown by Lt(jg) Tom Killefer. The aircraft was pictured on Nissan Island (in the Green Island group) following a forced landing due to engine failure on 5 March 1944. The aircraft bears what look likes five kill marks, but the scoreboard actually represents Killefer's 4.5 total (*National Archives*)

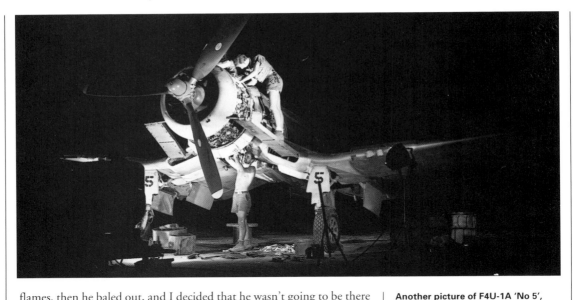

flames, then he baled out, and I decided that he wasn't going to be there to get us the next day. I came around and tried to boresight him – I did actually fire my guns but I was too close and I must have straddled him. He flashed by on his descent, and I swear he was shaking his fist at me as I almost ran into the canopy of his 'chute. I hauled ass and by the time I finally woke up and looked around there were three of his buddies right on my tail – one on each flank and one dead astern. Luckily, I was flying

Another picture of F4U-1A 'No 5', this time being worked on by Marine mechanics at Bougainville on 8 February 1944. VF-17 were one of the few Corsair squadrons to assign aircraft to individual pilots, each machine having a number between '1' and '36' which helped to distinguish individual flights within a squadron, numbers '1' to '4' making up the first flight and so on. For a time the aircraft also had their spinners and first 18 inches of their props painted in different colours to denote each flight – Blackburn's flight were marked with red, Hedrick's white and so on. This practice was soon abandoned, however, as the system proved impractical to sustain in combat due to aircraft losses and poor serviceability (*USMC*)

VF-17 pilots pose in front of the squadron scoreboard in January 1944. Standing, from left to right, are Lt Harry A 'Dirty Eddie' March, Jr (4 victories with VF-17 and 1 with VF-6), Lt(jg) Carl W Gilbert (1 victory) and Lt Walter J Schub (4.25 with VF-17 and 2 with VF-10). Kneeling are Lt(jg) Whitney C Wharton (2 victories with VF-10), Ens Frank A Jagger (2 victories) and Lt(jg) Harold J Bitzegaio (2 victories) (*Hedrick Collection*)

one of the new planes that we had picked up from Espiritu which was equipped with water injection that added about 25 hp – a few more knots of speed. Every time I saw one of them fire I could only change my altitude so as not to lose my speed. I gradually pulled away from them, and although they seemed to chase me forever, it actually wasn't more than ten minutes. I made it back to celebrate another day.

'On another occasion I was diving on somebody and he went into a snap roll. Lord knows what his thinking was, but it simply allowed me to catch up with him faster. It didn't bother me a bit as he was jiving around right there in front of me. That same flight I got another one that did the same thing. Maybe the section leader had decided that this might be a great tactic, but it didn't work too well. The Corsair was good at rolling and was a very stable gun platform – it could dive-bomb and so forth. I've flown the Hellcat and you'd be busy cranking on your tabs all the way down as torque and forces change, but with the Corsair there was very little, if any of that. You could whip it back and forth very easily. I know that I pulled over 9gs a few times. Our aeroplanes had accelerometers – a secret design in those days – and I once saw it register 11gs, although that wasn't in combat. It was when we were withdrawing from Rabaul covering the landings on Green Island and there was no opposition on the mission. Again as top cover, on the way back we encountered clouds above Empress August Bay. Usually in the afternoons in the Solomons there would be about 200 miles of thunderheads stretching across the area – hot and humid weather. Flying at about 2000 to 3000 ft, I looked at the clouds and decided to climb above them. If you got down on the water, which we had to do regularly, you had to sometimes fly about 15 ft above the water if you were to keep any type of contact at all. And then you'd be wondering where each little island was, as you could never be certain exactly where you were – we had no navigational aids at all. Unfortunately we got into the vortex at the top of the thunderhead, and all six of us were going in all directions, with wind shears taking us up and down, and that's where I got that 11gs. We all managed to get back safely, but it was by the grace of God on that one!'

War-weary F4U-1A Corsairs of VF-17 arrive back in the US on 7 August 1944 following their service in the Solomons. These aircraft would be overhauled and then used by a training squadron. From left to right is Killefer's 'No 5', Strieg's 'No 3' and an anonymous 'No 38' (*National Archives*)

SUCCESS IN THE SOUTH WEST

Following the American seizure of New Georgia, landings were made at Cape Torokina, Bougainville. on 1 November 1943. At that time there were four Marine Corsair units available to support the assault, namely VMFs -211, -212, -215, and -221. Bougainville, together with Green Island and Emirau (secured at later dates) helped to form a ring which enabled the strangulation of Rabaul, the main bastion of Japanese defence on New Britain, situated in the Bismarck archipelago. Airpower was used to neutralise the stronghold's air defences and to attack its lines of supply.

1st Lt Phillip C DeLong served with VMF-212, gaining his first two victories – a pair of Zekes – over Tobera airfield, New Britain, on 9 January 1944. His last three kills took place on 15 February against a formation of D3A *Val* dive-bombers, and here he describes the latter action.

'We covered the landings at Green Island on 15 February 1944, getting there just as the day was breaking. The ships were down below and then I saw the *Vals* – there were 15 of them. They were dive-bombers equipped with a rear seat gunner. I saw them starting quite high and rolling in. I couldn't see any sense in letting them get down to the ships, so I pulled in behind them. I got a good view of the gunner and shot him up. Then the aeroplane blew up. I got another two of them. My wingman had an armament fuse missing. Unable to use his guns all he did was go along for the ride!

'We strafed everything; trucks, barges, boats, natives in coconut trees, etc. Our guns were set up to fire at a fixed point where the bullets from all six guns would meet. If you got too close you didn't hit anything, but after the bullets had passed through the fixed point they would, in effect fan out in a large cone. This enabled you to spray a pretty large area.

'I was credited with 11.166 kills, the shared kills being split between three of us – Maj Hugh Elwood (5.166 kills), 1st Lt Allan Harrison and I. On 23 January, over Keravi Bay, Elwood made a run on a Zero and smoked him. I pulled up firing and got some flame out of him. Har-

F4U-1A 'No 777', BuNo 17777, following a landing accident at Bougainville on 14 December 1943. 1st Lt Phillip C DeLong had previously flown this aircraft on four of his missions during November. The machine wears a three-tone scheme with a stencilled number forward of the national insignia. The marking on the wing has been applied in the early style adopted in-theatre, with locally painted white bars. The tape applied forward of the canopy was used to seal the fuselage fuel tank access panels in order to stop fumes from entering the cockpit (*USMC*)

rison pulled up and managed to blow him up. Minutes later the same thing happened for the next plane up, so we split two kills between three of us. That same afternoon I shared another kill with Elwood.'

VICTORY CLAIMS

With the benefit of hindsight (and official Japanese loss records captured after the war) it has been established that the enemy lost less aircraft in air combat than the Allied forces had actually claimed to have destroyed. For example, in the two-month period 17 December 1943 to 19 February 1944 (the Imperial Navy's 11th Air Fleet was withdrawn on 20 February), the Allies claimed the destruction of 730 aircraft. By contrast, the Japanese Navy lost around 400 aircraft to all causes during the period. The Japanese Army Air Forces fared equally as badly, some units being totally annihilated during the campaign. Vast numbers of Japanese aircraft did not even see air combat, being destroyed on the ground by air attack. Figures cannot be accurately assessed but it can be estimated that the Allies claimed roughly twice the amount actually destroyed. This discrepancy is remarkably accurate compared to claims made in other theatres. Over claiming usually occurred during air combat and can largely be attributed to the confusion of battle. Claim inaccuracies and aircraft recognition mistakes are of little consequence compared to the overall results achieved. During the Solomons campaign the Japanese were to suffer such enormous losses that their Air Forces were, from then on, virtually incapable of taking on the Allied forces with the hope of achieving any kind of strategic success in air combat. It was because of these losses that the Japanese would later have to resort to suicide attacks in order to try and halt the American advance.

The Corsair units in the Solomons produced the highest scoring aces on the type during the whole conflict. Lt Robert M Hanson scored 25 victories with VMFs -214 and -215, before being killed in action on 3 February 1944 – he was posthumously awarded the Medal of Honor for kills achieved on 1 November 1943 and January 24 1944. Maj Gregory Boyington, commanding VMF-214, added to his previous six claims whilst flying with the 'Flying Tigers' in China, scoring 22 victories in the Corsair. He was awarded the Medal of Honor for actions on 17 October 1943, but was shot down and captured on 3 January 1944. Lt Kenneth A Walsh scored 20 victories whilst serving with VMF-124, being awarded the Medal of Honor in February 1944. He claimed his 21st, and final, victory on 22 June 1945 whilst serving with VMF-222. Capt Donald N Aldrich of VMF-215 achieved 20 victories, his last kill being scored on 9 February 1944. Capt Wilbur J Thomas of VMF-213 scored 16.5 victories during this campaign, before claiming a further two with the same unit on 16 February 1945, thus bringing his total claims to 18.5. VF-17 produced the Navy's top scoring ace of the theatre in the form of Lt Ira C Kepford, who was credited with 16 victories.

Three weather-beaten RNZAF F4U-1As are parked up between missions on Guadalcanal in mid-1944. By the time this shot was taken the threat of Japanese air attacks had subsided to the point where squadrons were confident that they could park lines of aircraft out in the open, rather than have them individually hidden away amongst the palm trees in revetments. The three-digit fin tip code was taken from the last three numbers in the aircraft's individual serial – 'No 393', for example, was actually NZ5393 (*via Jim Sullivan*)

RNZAF F4Us

Rabaul was deemed too difficult a target to attack by direct assault and was thus allowed to 'wither on the vine'. Following the destruction of Japanese air strength in the Solomons and Bismarcks, Navy and Marine Corsair units continued to harass the Japanese strongpoint by attacking ground targets. The Japanese evacuated the last of their shattered air-power on 20 February 1944. The Americans were joined by Royal New Zealand Air Force (RNZAF) units equipped with the Corsair at Bougainville on 14 May 1944 – the first unit to arrive was No 20 Sqn. Veterans of the P-40 Kittyhawk in the Solomons in 1943/44, these Kiwi units brought experience to the front, having gained a total of 99 aerial victories against the Japanese in operations to date. By the time the Corsairs arrived, however, enemy airpower in the Solomons was almost non-existent, and the RNZAF was unable to achieve any further aerial victories. Not to be deterred, they made their contribution to the war effort in the South Pacific by carrying out escort and ground attack missions in the area, which ended only in August 1945 with the final Japanese surrender.

A total of 13 RNZAF units received Corsairs in 1944/45, being numbered between 14 and 26. Spread across the South Pacific, these units utilised the F4U-1A, -1D and FG-1D versions of the Chance Vought/Goodyear fighter. Of the 424 airframes issued to the Kiwis (364 -1As/-1Ds and 60 FG-1Ds), no less than 150 (35 per cent) were lost, although only 17 of these were officially credited to enemy action. Squadrons were rotated into the frontline for three-month tours from bases in New Zealand, pools of aircraft being left at frontline strips by out-going squadrons for use by their replacements. Unlike the British, who disposed of their massed ranks of Corsairs almost immediately after World War 2 (see the Fleet Air Arm chapter for details), the RNZAF valued their aircraft, and kept several units in service with the FG-1Ds particularly. The last unit flying the Corsair in the frontline was No 14 Sqn, who performed occupation duty with their FG-1Ds in Japan until the Allies pulled out in October 1948. Following the wind down of the squadron, the Corsairs – all weary veterans of war – were unceremoniously piled together and burnt, thus abruptly ending the RNZAF's association with the Chance Vought fighter.

Three-letter codes were rarely seen on Kiwi Corsairs, with this formation boasting a mix of combinations which perhaps denotes the presence of three separate squadrons within this strike force, seen heading for its target in early 1945 (*via Jim Sullivan*)

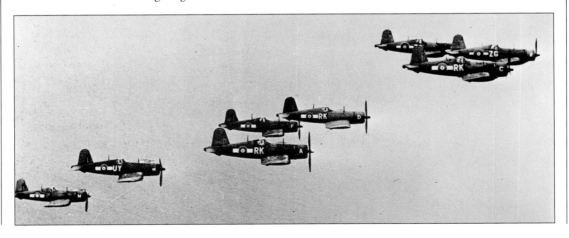

BRITISH CORSAIRS

Thanks to a less than impressive range of fighter and attack aircraft on offer from dedicated naval manufacturers like Fairey and Blackburn, the Fleet Air Arm (FAA) was forced to turn to fleet-modified RAF fighters in the form of the Sea Hurricane and Seafire to initially re-equip its carrier air wings during the dark days of 1941-42. Although both of these types were a great improvement over the Fulmar and Skua, neither boasted a truly sufficient range to operate at distance from the task force, or possessed truly sound deck landing characteristics.

Fortunately for the FAA's hard-pressed naval aviators, the first examples of a true carrier-bred fighter in the form of the Grumman Wildcat (Martlet) had begun to reach Britain in serious numbers by late 1941. Here was an aircraft that had a more than adequate range, was docile in the landing pattern and could hold its own in combat – its only real drawback was a rather modest top speed of 315 mph. Nevertheless, it was quickly accepted by the Navy, who in turn cast an envious eye westward across the Atlantic in search of a machine to supplement the Wildcat.

At about that time the Chance Vought company of Connecticut was putting its radical new fleet fighter – the XF4U-1 Corsair – through its paces prior to delivery to the US Navy. Wickedly quick, this machine became the target for a lend-lease deal between the British and American governments. Indeed, so popular was the 'bent-winged bird' that no less than 2012 Corsairs, divided into four marks, were eventually utilised by the FAA, which gave the aircraft the distinction of being the most populous US type to see service with the Royal Navy in World War 2.

Over the years much has been said about the aircraft's 'sporting' handling characteristics around a carrier deck, with pilots' opinions seemingly divided according to their own experiences of the Corsair. Senior US naval aviators were convinced that the F4U-1 was too difficult an aircraft for the average pilot to master in 1942, possessing incipient bounce due to overly stiff oleos, a tendency to torque stall without warning and a poor view over the nose during landing approach.

These factors resulted in carrier-based US Navy units being almost exclusively equipped with the docile Hellcat until the F4U was finally cleared for deck ops in late 1944 – by this stage FAA Corsair units had accrued almost a year's flat top experience, as well as having seen combat from carriers in both Europe and the Pacific since April 1944.

Never phased by the aircraft's 'wild' reputation, the British went

Fresh off the 'boat' from the US, a recently arrived Corsair II is taxied gingerly along the Peri track at an anonymous airfield in Britain in early 1944, its wings askew. The pilot's head can just be seen behind the cowling flaps as he leans out the cockpit in order to see what is ahead of him. Lurking in the winter mist behind the Corsair is a solitary Swordfish, plus a pair of Martlets. Despite its ascendancy over all previous FAA fighters, not all naval aviators in the Senior Service were enamoured with the Corsair, as Capt Eric 'Winkle' Brown attests to in the following quote. 'Oddly enough, the Royal Navy was not quite so fastidious as the US Navy regarding deck landing characteristics, and cleared the Corsair for deck operation some nine months before its American counterpart. The obstacles to the Corsair's shipboard use were admittedly not insurmountable, but I can only surmise that the apparently ready acceptance by their Lordships of the Admiralty of the Chance Vought fighter for carrier operation must have been solely due to the exigencies of the time, for the landing behaviour of the Corsair really was bad' (*via Phil Jarrett*)

Having completed the landing on cycle, deck crews busily manhandle a trio of Corsairs into their appropriate spots under the watchful gaze of a clutch of senior officers in the middle of the photograph. Both the carrier and the unit are sadly unknown, although the '7' code denotes that the Corsairs belong to one of the many training squadrons equipped with the type in 1944. Standing behind the cockpit of '7T', map in hand, is the carrier's Commander (Flying), who had just flown one of the aircraft aboard (*via Aeroplane*)

about re-equipping with the Corsair I from mid-1943 onwards, squadrons being trained for 'blue water' ops from the word go. Subtle mods to the aircraft included the clipping of the wings by eight inches due to the smaller confines of the hangar decks on British carriers. This change in span brought with it the unexpected bonus of improved sink rate, thus partially eradicating the aircraft's propensity for 'floating' in the final stages of landing. However, despite this mod some senior FAA pilots expressed fears akin to their American cousins.

Nevertheless, by early 1944 eight units had been formed expressly for carrier operations with both the Home and Far East fleets – this number would eventually reach a staggering 18 units by VJ-Day. The original F4U-1 'birdcage', known as the Corsair I (95 delivered), was the initial version supplied to Nos 1830 and 1833 Sqns in the US, but none of these ever saw combat. This honour fell to the more definitive Mk II, an anglicised version of the F4U-1A that was delivered to the tune of 510 airframes. Work ups were complete by the end of 1943, and the Corsair IIs were loaded aboard escort carriers for shipment to Britain.

By April 1944 the Home Fleet felt confident enough to blood the Corsair II in combat, and 28 aircraft from Nos 1834 and 1836 Sqns duly provided top cover on the 3rd of that month as No 47 Naval Fighter Wing (FW) for Operation *Tungsten* – an air strike by six carriers (121 aircraft) on the German battleship *Tirpitz*. Part of HMS *Victorious*'s air wing, the Corsair pilots encountered no enemy aircraft during the dawn raid, and returned to the carrier without having had their combined mettle tested – the Corsair's contribution to the war against Germany was restricted to supporting Home Fleet strikes against this target through to August.

The Corsair's combat debut in the Indian Ocean took place concurrently with the first *Tirpitz* strike in April 1944, although the former action was a far less orchestrated affair than *Tungsten*. Nos 1830 and 1833 Sqns, who formed No 15 FW aboard HMS *Illustrious*, were used to sweep the area east of Ceylon clean of commerce raiders, and although little real combat was met, it did give the FAA a chance to operate closely with the US Navy in the form of USS *Saratoga*, and her embarked air wing.

The Corsair force in-theatre effectively doubled in July with the arrival of *Victorious*. No 1837 Sqn also arrived in Ceylon to join *Illustrious*, increasing the embarked strength per vessel to 42 Corsair IIs each, split evenly between a trio of units. This enlarged force got the chance to show its worth on 25 July when Sabang Island was hit, although the Corsairs took a backseat to three battleships, seven cruisers and two destroyers which shelled the port and oil storage site.

Whilst covering the force withdrawal, a trio of units were given the chance to blood the Corsair in aerial combat when a handful of enemy aircraft attempted to attack the warships. No 1830 Sqn claimed three Zekes, whilst fellow No 15 FW unit No 1833 Sqn downed two Zekes and a Ki 21 *Sally* bomber. Finally, the sole kill to fall to *Victorious* was yet another Zeke, which was destroyed by a Corsair from the temporarily-assigned No 1838 Sqn. Aside from being the FAA's first of nearly 50 kills in the Corsair, these successes were also the first deck-based victories for the fighter, although its land-based score was nearing four figures after 17 months in combat with the USMC and Navy.

After more aerially unopposed target strikes, Corsair pilots again encountered the enemy in the skies over the Car Nicobar Islands in October 1944, although this time only *Victorious*'s units flew the Corsair flag. A handful of *Oscars* defending the islands were downed in the one-sided duels that took place, seven Army fighters being downed for the loss of two Corsairs and a Hellcat. Canadian Lt Leslie Durno, of No 1834 Sqn, claimed four of this total, destroying one fighter single-handedly and sharing three with his wingman – some confusion exists as to the correct identity of this pilot as a Scot by the name of Lt Alec Durno was also reportedly serving with No 1834 Sqn as Senior Pilot at this time!

One last operation was performed by the Corsair in this theatre on 4 January 1945 when *Victorious* operated in support of the strike on the refinery at Pangkalan Brandan, again on Sumatra – this raid was viewed as a dress rehearsal for the bigger Palembang strike three weeks later. The pilots of No 47 FW were tasked with providing top cover (along with *Indefatigable*'s Seafire F IIIs) for the Avengers, and duly ran into a force of *Oscars*, as well as a handful of *Dinah* recce aircraft and *Sally* bombers. Twelve aircraft were downed for the loss a single Avenger, with seven of these kills falling to Corsair pilots – Lt Durno shared a *Dinah* and a *Sally*, whilst No 1836 Sqn's Sub Lt Don Sheppard (also a Canadian) claimed two *Oscars* as the unit downed five Nakajima fighters.

With the creation of the British Pacific Fleet (BPF) in January 1945, the Royal Navy moved its force from Trincomalee to Sydney, and en route to their new home, senior staff officers decided to make use of the massed ranks of four large fleet carriers to hit the sprawling ex-Shell refinery at Pladjoe, near Palembang in Sumatra – this raid had been planned since early December 1944. Codenamed *Meridian One* and *Two*, 144 sorties were launched on 24 January, followed by more raids five days later – the former attack was the second largest force put up by the FAA in World War 2. Included in the first strike were 32 Corsairs from *Illustrious* and *Victorious*, performing bomber escort duties (16 close in with the bombers and an equal number flying as top cover), and a further 24 on a *Ramrod* sweep of the local airfields.

Flak took a heavy toll of the *Ramrod* raiders, who failed to prevent the Japanese *Tojos*, *Nicks* and *Oscars* from launching against the main strike force. Five Corsairs were lost, but in return 34 Japanese aircraft were destroyed on the ground – little evidence of the enemy in the air on these

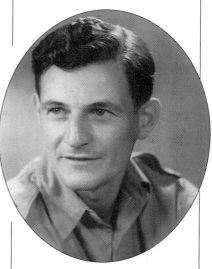

Solitary Royal Marine ace of World War 2, then Maj (later Lieutenant Colonel) Ronnie Hay enjoyed a remarkably successful combat career flying all manner of FAA fighters, including both the Skua and Fulmar I. After scoring kills in both these less than impressive fleet fighters, Hay revelled in the power and manoeuvrability of the Corsair, stating that 'for the first time in four years of war we were on top in combat – the masters of the air – as no others could touch us, and that made our morale "Ace High"' (*Ronnie Hay*)

The early morning storm clouds that have left puddles on HMS *Victorious*'s steel deck are left behind as the carrier steams on towards the East Indies. Sailors can be picked out between massed ranks of Corsair IIs from Nos 1834 and 1836 Sqns, preparing the aircraft for their next strike on Sumatra in January 1945. The Corsairs wearing a number '7' on their starboard undercarriage door and a letter on the opposing oleo are from No 1834 Sqn, whilst those with '8A' to 'T' on both gear legs are from No 1836 (*via Phil Jarrett*)

attacks meant that the escorting Corsairs were the only ones to engage in combat. Over 20 Army fighters attacked the force, but the Corsair pilots flying top cover were well up to the task at hand and claimed eight for the loss of a single No 1833 Sqn Corsair (downed by a *Tojo*) in a battle fought around the edge of the Avengers.

Leading scorer with an *Oscar* and a *Tojo* on this sortie was veteran Marine ace, Maj (later Lieutenant Colonel) Ronnie Hay, who was serving as Wing Leader of No 47 Wg at the time. A frontline FAA fighter pilot since 1939, Hay had scored a shared kill in Skuas in 1940 during the Battle of Norway with No 801 Sqn from *Ark Royal*, followed by seven individual or shared victories in the Mediterranean in 1941 as part of Force 'H' in Fulmar Is with No 808 Sqn, again aboard the *Ark*.

His role in the Palembang strikes was a unique one for he was designated the Air Co-ordinator, which meant he oversaw all the various strike formations as they hit the refinery at their schedules times from a variety of directions as briefed – Hay had been one of the few FAA pilots sent by the Navy on the RAF's exclusive Wing Leader course at Charmy Down in April 1943 Full bottle on the etiquette of massed air strikes, he was despatched to the Mediterranean to lecture on the subject, before being sent to Ceylon as Commander Flying at China Bay. With the arrival of the Corsair in-theatre in early 1944, Hay sensed that the former 'back water' of a conflict in the Far East was at last being viewed with the seriousness it deserved, so he duly wangled his way out from behind a desk back onto operational flying, and was adopted by *Victorious*, who welcomed both his combat experience and strike tactics background. Palembang at last saw him putting theory in to practice on a grand scale.

The strike went on for some while, and during this time Hay, and his flight of three other pilots (including the FAA's sole all-Corsair ace of the conflict, Canadian Sub Lt Don Sheppard) drawn predominantly from No 1836 Sqn, patrolled as an integral flight between the Corsairs of the strike force and those flying top cover. Hay was flying his field-modified Corsair II JT427 – appropriately coded 'TRH' – which boasted oblique and vertical cameras to enable him to record views of the target for post-strike evaluation (Hay was also a graduate of the RAF's photographic interpretation course at Benson, where he had learned to fly high altitude vertical line overlap missions, and thereby achieve the most accurate post-strike evaluation photographs). Indeed, all four of his kills in Corsairs were scored in this machine, and due to its special fit it was probably the only one of its type aboard either *Victorious* or *Illustrious* assigned to one pilot. Hay reflects on this mission, and the Corsair in general in this theatre, in the following interview, undertaken specially for this volume.

'With the Corsair you felt like were literally strapped into an armchair in your sitting room, the cockpit was that large. You honestly felt like a "king" sitting up there, with virtually unlimited visibility through the bubble canopy of the Mark II. We flew those aircraft very hard, and just to illustrate this point, a little after the Sumatra show we ventured northward to Okinawa for *Iceberg*, where I came across an airfield full of the latest spec F4U-4s in glossy sea blue at Manus, in the Admiralty Islands, awaiting shipment back to the US. I came across the US Navy Officer in charge of this operation and asked him what was occurring. He told me that they were being returned to the 'States for overhaul and repair prior to being sent to the frontline again. I enquired as to their individual service use per airframe and he replied that they had seen about 500 hours of flying each. I was astonished, and replied that our Corsair IIs had accrued nearly 2000 each and were no nearer an overhaul or deep service than the day they were built! I ventured a swap whereby I took one of his non-serviced machines in place of my old crate, and he replied, "Sure bud, you can have any one you like. Any guy going up to the "sharp end" can take anything he wants!" Sadly, I fear my admiral would have spotted the F4U-4's glossy blue scheme sat amongst the ranks of sea grey Corsair IIs on *Victorious*!

'Returning to Palembang, all the Corsairs despatched to the target carried drop tanks which gave a maximum of five hours flight time. We used the external fuel first, and jettisoned them as soon as we got into action. I had my own four-aircraft flight adopt a loose formation over the target, with Sheppard to my rear. We sauntered around checking on where the Japs were, and how they were responding to the raid in progress.

'The first strike on the refineries was a bit hit and miss in terms of targets destroyed, and because of the sheer number of aircraft involved, my ability to co-ordinate formations of Avenger IIs, Firefly Is, Hellcat Is, Corsairs IIs and Seafire F IIIs was rather limited, particularly after the fuel dumps were hit and the site became obscured in dense black smoke. I therefore moved my flight into a position where we could protect the Avengers should enemy fighters show up. The next thing I knew a *Tojo* came flashing past my bows hell bent on attacking the bombers, and I quickly lined him up in my sights and fired a two-second burst in his direction. I must have hit a fuel tank because the aircraft blew up. An *Oscar* was spotted soon afterwards and I led the flight down after him to jungle level, but unlike the *Tojo* he refused to burn, instead crashing into the ground at high speed.

'Five days later, in the immediate aftermath of *Meridian Two*, I was attempting to perform a series of post-strike vertical line overlap photographic passes on the refinery site when we ran into a mixed flight of

Once airborne the squadrons would be tasked with providing fighter cover for Avenger IIs and Firefly Is, one unit sticking close by the vulnerable bombers, whilst the second squadron would patrol at height above the formation. This impressive view shows aircraft of No 6 FW being lead by Maj Ronnie Hay on a formation flypast of RNAS Colombo, Ceylon, in May 1944. The Corsairs are wearing a mix of codes and odd-sized national markings (*Ronnie Hay*)

Corsair II JT422 is typical of the 36 Chance Vought fighters that made up No 47 FW aboard HMS *Victorious* in 1944/45. The two-letter code of No 1836 Sqn is clearly visible, as is the crudely chalked on letter T to the left of the number 8 – all squadron machines eventually had this second letter painted on by the time of the Palembang raid in late January 1945. Its paint lustreless and stained, JT422 was being flown on this occasion by a Lt Knight (*Ronnie Hay*)

four *Tojos* and *Oscars*. This immediately stopped the recce work, and Sheppard and I quickly despatched one of each for two half-kills apiece. In combating the Jap fighters you simply used your superior speed to make solitary diving passes at them, restricting the temptation to turn with them at all cost. We enjoyed such a speed advantage over both types it was pointless slowing down in order to try and dogfight.'

Having fought long and hard for a 'piece of the action' in the Pacific, the Royal Navy was determined to up a good showing, which in turn meant tough escort and strafing sorties for the units – Nos 1830 and 1833 on *Illustrious*, Nos 1834 and 1836 on *Victorious* and Nos 1841 and 1842 Sqns on *Formidable*. Typical squadron strength throughout the eight months of combat in 1945 was 18 Corsair IIs, although with the arrival of *Formidable* in April the Goodyear-built Mk IV made its combat debut.

Returning briefly to the *Meridian* strikes on the Pladjoe refineries for the final time, aside from Hay and Sheppard's single kills, a further three aircraft were shared between Nos 1830 and 1834 Sqns. However, Lt Durno, who had scored one and four shared kills all in Corsair, was one of two pilots lost on the raid – he was shot down attacking an airfield and captured. Sadly, he was beheaded in Changi prison in August 1945, along with several other FAA aircrew downed in the Palembang raid.

After a spell in Sydney, the BPF joined forces with the US Fifth Fleet to form Task Force 57, and of the 270 FAA aircraft (split between five carriers) contributed to the force 110 of them were Corsairs. The battle for Okinawa, codenamed *Iceberg*, was the BPF's first Pacific combat proper, and commencing 26 March strikes were launched against Sakishima Gunto. Aside from flak suppression and strike work, Corsair units were kept busy repelling *kamikazes*, as Ronnie Hay witnessed at first hand.

'The biggest aerial threat to life posed by the Japanese came in the form of *kamikaze* attacks in the final months of the war. We experienced some

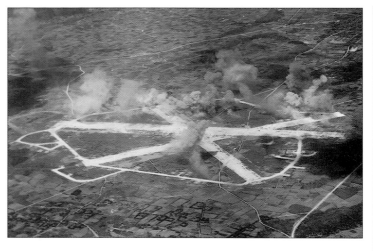

Typical of the shots taken by Ronnie Hay in his specially-modified recce-Corsair II, this view shows the Japanese airfield on the island of Miyako, in the Sakishima Gunto chain, under attack by FAA Avenger IIs and Corsair IIs in March 1945. During the raids the Navy bombers concentrated on cratering the runways, thus restricting the airfield's use as a staging post for aircraft being flown into Okinawa from Formosa (*Ronnie Hay*)

Another strafing mission over, pilots of Nos 1834 and 1836 Sqns head for the crewroom in line abreast formation. The pilot third from the right is Canadian Lt Don Sheppard, the only all-Corsair ace the FAA produced in World War 2 (*Ronnie Hay*)

very unpleasant moments with carrier decks full of bombed up and fuelled aircraft waiting to turn into wind before being cleared to launch. I can remember sitting there in my aircraft as the deck slowly healed over, moments away from take-off, when all of a sudden the ship's guns would open up and I would crane my neck skywards searching for a Zeke or a *Val* hell bent on burying itself in the bowels of the carrier. I can remember sitting in the cockpit watching one *kamikaze* just miss the *"Indom"* which was about to launch her air wing less than half a mile away from us. I was first off, fortunately, and as soon as the signal was given I was gone, followed by my flight – pity the poor sods behind us!'

Ten Japanese aircraft were claimed by Corsairs during these attacks – which lasted till mid-April – split evenly between *Victorious* and *Illustrious*. Entering the fray once again on 4 May, the BPF Corsairs intercepted a formation of 20 assorted enemy aircraft as they attacked the carrier force. Amongst the defenders was Don Sheppard, who downed a *Judy* to achieve ace status – three other aircraft were claimed by *Victorious*'s Corsairs. The following day a Corsair IV from the recently arrived No 1841 Sqn shot down a Zeke to claim *Formidable*'s first aerial kill.

Eventually, after a month of strikes the defenders of Okinawa were beaten, but not before much damage had been inflicted on Task Force 57's carriers – two-thirds of the 270 aircraft despatched from Sydney had been destroyed or damaged, a large percentage through *kamikaze* attacks. Following a spell of R&R, the carriers returned to the war zone for the last time in July, with Corsair units employed predominantly on *Ramrod* strikes on airfields as all aerial opposition had by now gone. Indeed, only two more kills were scored prior to VJ Day, and both fell to No 1841 Sqn – a *Kate* was claimed at the end of July, followed by a *Grace* on 9 August.

Later that momentous day, just when it appeared that the final FAA act with the Corsair had been played, a veteran Canadian flight commander from No 1841 Sqn by the name of Lt Robert Hampton Gray made the ultimate sacrifice during a shipping strike on the Honshu coast. Hit by flak, he nevertheless closed to within 50 ft of his target – a trademark approach he had used time and again firstly in the Norwegian campaign in April 1944, and then throughout *Formidable*'s final weeks of war against mainland Japan. This time luck was not on his side and he was lost in the resulting explosion when his target blew up. Gray was awarded a posthumous VC – only the second naval pilot to receive Britain's highest military award in World War 2.

Thus ended the FAA's Corsair war. Of the 18 squadrons eventually equipped with the type, 8 saw combat. Only two of the four marks operated by the FAA were used in action, and of the 2000+ received, roughly 40 remained in service until August 1946.

Victorious **despatched Corsair II/IVs and Avenger IIs on strikes to the Japanese mainland up until 11 August 1945. With her aircrew suffering fatigue, and her supplies running low, the carrier was 'chopped', along with the bulk of the BPF's Task Force 38, and ordered to return to Sydney. Prior to departure, the vessel was resupplied at sea (RAS) by fleet support vessels, and this shot was taken soon after this had taken place. Parked on the deck amongst the Corsairs and Avengers is a solitary No 1701 Sqn Sea Otter (***Ronnie Hay***)**

THE CENTRAL PACIFIC

Whilst land-based units had carried out most of the work in the South West Pacific the vast Central Pacific theatre became primarily the preserve of the carriers. Corsairs were, however, based on various islands in the Pacific, and these units were mainly required to attack enemy units by-passed by the carriers during the island hopping campaign. Marine F4Us carried on the effort in the Gilbert and Marshall Islands for instance, with the majority of missions flown here being of the ground attack variety – there were very few Japanese aircraft left operating in these areas by now. It was here that the Corsair would perfect its new ground attack role, first developed in the Solomons, which would be put to good use as the Americans advanced towards Japan.

The Marine F4Us also missed out to a large extent on the air combat associated with the occupation of the Marianas, aircraft (Hellcats mainly) from TF-58 destroying some 200 enemy fighters gathered on Saipan and Tinian in what became known as the 'Marianas Turkey Shoot'. Land-based units in this theatre would, however, see more aerial engagements with the advent of the Philippines campaign, where they would fly CAP missions for the carriers taking part in the invasion of Leyte in October 1944. Marine Corsair units would go on to help with the liberation of the Philippines by launching ground attack missions in support of the advancing forces. As the campaign progressed Adm Chester Nimitz's fast carriers would continue the drive into the Central Pacific.

VF-17 had first demonstrated the Corsair to be suitable for carrier operations before their final deployment as a land-based unit. They had worked with Chance Vought technicians to improve the Corsair's shortcomings, and the resulting improvements helped to convince the Bureau of Aeronautics of its worth – the F4U was cleared for carrier use in April 1944. By that time, however, the availability of the F6F had led to the latter's widespread use by the fast carrier fleet, instead of the more versatile Corsair.

The first US Navy Corsair combat deployment aboard a carrier began on 9 January 1944 with USS *Enterprise*. VF(N)-101 (actually the second half of VF(N)-75, left behind in late 1943 because of equipment delays), equipped with

The first US Navy Corsair deployment began on 9 January 1944 when VF(N)-101, commanded by Lt Cdr Richard E Harmer, boarded USS *Enterprise* as part of Air Group 10. Equipped with F4U-2 night-fighters, the unit was tasked with defending the fleet against Japanese attacks at night. VF(N)-101 was credited with the destruction of five enemy aircraft, one probable and three damaged. Here, an F4U-2 is raised to the deck in the late afternoon, whilst VF-10 Hellcats can be seen in the background (*National Archives via Pete Mersky*)

four F4U-2s, beginning operations as part of Air Group Ten whilst under the command of Lt Cdr Richard E 'Chick' Harmer (formerly the XO of VF(N)-75, Harmer was an F4F Guadalcanal vet, having served with VF-3 aboard *Saratoga* in 1942). A second four-Corsair VF(N)-101 det was also established aboard *Intrepid* with Air Wing Six at this time. *Enterprise*'s first night interception took place on 19 February 1944.

Operating from a carrier at night is possibly the most difficult task that a Naval aviator has to perform. This being so, it was ironic that the US Navy first ushered the 'unruly' Corsair into fleet service in this role, particularly when one considers staff attitudes towards the aircraft. Night-fighter variants of the F4U also served with land-based VMF(N)-532, commanded by Maj Everett Vaughn, and VF(N)-75 led by Lt Cdr William J Widhelm. In total these units were to be credited with 14 aircraft destroyed, 4 probables and 3 damaged.

Marine Corsair carrier deployments were a direct response to Japanese suicide strikes against Allied naval targets. The *kamikaze* attacks began in strength during the Leyte invasion that took place in late October 1944, and although this form of attack was born out of desperation, it appeared to the Japanese to be very effective. Even though they greatly overestimated the results of their attacks, they were nevertheless inflicting serious damage. *Kamikaze* attacks only occurred for a short period, but were to become the cause of over one-fifth of all sinkings and almost half the damage sustained by American shipping during the whole of World War 2.

There was only one way for the Americans to defend themselves from the new menace, and that was through increased fighter cover. The Navy needed as many fighters as it could get, and the carriers from which to operate them from. However, they simply did not have enough pilots to meet the requirement as their training programme had been cut back as the tide of the conflict had turned globally – therefore, the Marines were called in to fill the gap. Marine aviators began carrier training in the summer of 1944 at the beginning of the CVE programme. The plan was for them to operate Corsairs from escort carriers, their operational emphasis being based on supporting Marine Ground Forces. However, the first Marines actually deployed on board the big fleet carriers – ten squadrons eventually saw deck service during 1945. The urgent Navy requirement for extra fighters again meant that F4U pilots were committed to the combat theatre with insufficient training, and

F4U-1A 'No 122' of VMF-111 was the only aircraft to receive an official award for its combat service during World War 2. Operating from the Gilbert and Marshall Islands, the aircraft is pictured with 100 mission marks to denote the number of sorties it completed with the same engine – it never had to turn back due to mechanical trouble. VMF-111, along with other land-based units, was tasked with the destruction of by-passed Japanese garrisons, and saw very little air-to-air combat (*via Phil Jarrett*)

F4U-1As of VMF-222 on Samar in the Philippines. The unit was based here from January 1945 until it moved to Okinawa on 22 May. This aircraft is adorned with the emblem of the Navy's Construction Battalions, the SEABEEs, who were responsible for the construction of all their airfields. The unit was credited with destroying 51 enemy aircraft and 20 probables in the South West Pacific, and gained a further two kills whilst based on Okinawa (*USMC*)

Capt Francis E 'Effie' Pierce of VMF-121 poses next to his FG-1A BuNo 14056, nicknamed *Mary* after his wife, on Peleliu on 18 November 1944. Pierce had claimed a total of six victories earlier in the South West Pacific – four in the Wildcat and one in a Corsair (the unit converted to the F4U in April 1943). VMF-121 claimed 204.5 kills in this theatre, the last occurring on 18 July 1943. Only one more was claimed – on 28 April 1945 a *Myrt* was destroyed near Ulithi. Whilst on Peleliu the unit flew mostly ground attack missions against Yap (*USMC*)

F4U-1Ds of VMFs -124 and -213 from *Essex* escort TBM Avengers on a strike against Formosa on 3 January 1945. This was the first Marine Corsair combat mission to be launched from a carrier, both F4Us and TBMs attacking Kagi airfield. Returning from the target Lt Col William A Millington, VMF-124's CO, destroyed a Japanese *Nick*, this being the unit's first kill of the cruise (*USMC*)

early sorties were marred by operational losses around the carrier.

VMFs -124 and -213 began deck ops soon after they returned to the Pacific equipped with 36 brand new F4U-1Ds in late 1944. The units boarded *Essex* as part of Task Force 38 at Ulithi on 28 December 1944, and launched their first combat sorties on 3 January 1945 when elements from both squadrons escorted TBMs attacking Kagi Airfield, on Formosa. Next they hit Okinawa, then the fleet moved down to the northern Philippines, attacking northern Luzon on 6/7 January. Passing through Luzon Strait, they sailed into the South China Sea, from where a massive strike was then launched against Saigon, in French Indochina, followed on the 16th by attacks against Hong Kong, Amoy, Swatow and Formosa again. Following a second strike on Okinawa, the fleet returned to Ulithi on 26 January. Adm Halsey was relieved by Spruance and the fleet set sail on 4 February as Task Force 58. This time the fleet boasted four large carriers – the *Bennington*, *Wasp*, *Essex* and *Bunker Hill*.

Each carrier was equipped with two Marine Corsair squadrons, whilst *Bunker Hill* also had the Navy's first day fighter Corsair squadron (VF-84, now commanded by VF-17's former XO, Roger Hedrick) embarked. The fleet was ready to attack the Japanese homeland for the first time. On 16/17 February they launched strikes against Japanese airfields, with the intention of destroying as many aircraft as possible so that they could not be used against the Iwo Jima invasion force. The fleet then travelled south and carried out attack sorties against 'Iwo' itself. They continued missions in support of the invasion until the 22nd, and then launched a strike against Chichi Jima. More sorties were flown against Japan on the 25th and Okinawa on 1 March, before the fleet returned to Ulithi.

Lt Col William A Millington, CO of both VMFs -124 and -213 claimed their first victory on 3 January 1945 whilst flying CAP during the initial Okinawa strikes. Six-kill ace Capt Howard Finn had earlier served with VMF-124 in the Solomons, and relates some of his experiences of the *kamikaze* period:

'I never had an accident either taking off or landing aboard a carrier, although landing at night was a pretty wild experience. The radar put you in position and then you would get into that imaginary cone at the rear of the ship. We would approach from the stern from two miles out until we picked up the little blue lights and then if our approach was correct they would turn on the meatball. We'd keep the meatball centred as you couldn't see the LSO and hopefully fly right in. In darkness, during bad weather it's the most precise flying you can do.

'We were warned about the *kamikazes* – indeed the *Essex* had been hit by one just before our cruise. We would have to shoot them down before reaching the fleet for it was their tactics that were doing the most damage. As a result, we abandoned defensive tactics when we went after the *kamikazes*. The Navy really feared the them, more so than on the Marines. They used destroyers as pickets and we

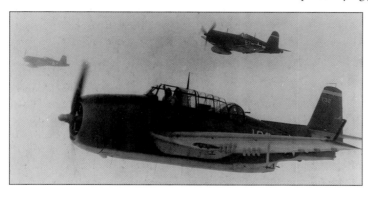

'Finn's Fools' pictured before a flight on board the *Essex* in December 1944. From left to right are Capt Edmond Hartsock (2 victories), 1st Lt George B Parker, standing, (1 victory), Capt Howard J Finn (6 victories) and 1st Lt William McGill (3 victories). Whilst on his first cruise with VMF-124, Finn increased his tally of five kills gained in the Solomons by downing an *Oscar* and sharing the credit for damaging another with 2nd Lt Don Carlson during a mission to Kumagaya airfield, in Japan, on 25 February 1945 (*Finn Collection*)

flew CAP over them. The *kamikazes* would go after the pickets, these being the first ships they came across. By the time of the Leyte and Okinawa operations they were no longer trying to establish air superiority, merely trying to destroy ships with *kamikaze* tactics.

'We hit the dock facilities at Formosa and we then strafed a destroyer that was later sunk by Navy planes. The destroyer tried to escape to the north, and after we had attacked it I flew over the vessel to take pictures. I had a camera in the side of my aeroplane and the plan was for me to photograph the ship in preparation for another strike. Just at that time a Navy plane must have hit the ship with a 1000-lb bomb because it sank within two minutes. We then flew raids against targets in Indochina, losing several pilots to AA. Joe Lynch was one of the pilots shot down, and he walked out of the jungle on foot. Both Okinawa and Taiwan were hit before we returned to Ulithi.

'We then supported the landings on Iwo Jima and then the fleet was sent north to attack Japan for four or five days, covering the airfields so that the enemy could not send down *kamikazes* to attack the invasion force. We were assigned airfields north of Tokyo. On the way in we kept seeing these aircraft drop down out of the clouds and then go back up. I took my flight around and waited for them to drop down. One appeared and I shot him down. Another one dropped down and we chased him until he flew into the side of a mountain.

'Our "Offensive Fighter Sweeps" against enemy airfields were conducted without external ordnance – we just used our guns. When attacking airfields we would go in *en masse* to dilute the anti-aircraft fire. Sometimes we would do a second sweep, depending on the defences, dividing the airfield up and each flight taking a different segment. Later, we conducted ground attack missions using rockets and bombs as well as our machine guns. At that time we also had the 20 mm cannon which was a more effective strafing weapon than the .50 cal gun, although they were not as reliable. They seemed to get jammed more often, and it was not uncommon to only have one of the four cannon able to fire. They were also prone to freezing at high altitude.'

Task Force 58 hit Japan again on 18 March, and this time the Navy had a lot more Corsairs available. *Essex* and *Wasp* had had their Marines replaced with Air Groups 83 and 86, both having F4U-equipped VBF squadrons. The fleet was enlarged with the addition of *Franklin* and *Intrepid*, sharing five Corsair squadrons between them, whilst the *Hancock*, with one, brought the total to 13 in all. When *Franklin* and *Wasp* were hit by air attack on the 19th this total was quickly reduced to nine. The fleet also acted in support of the Okinawa invasion, and from the

F4U-1D 'No 176' launches from USS *Bunker Hill* on 19 February 1945. Roger Hedrick commanded VF-84 until he assumed command of the Air Group following the death of the previous commander who was killed in action. He added two victories (*Frank*s) to his score with VF-17, bringing his final tally to twelve on 26 February 1945 while flying F4U-1D BuNo 57803 (*National Archives*)

Rocket-armed F4U-1D 'No 183' launches from *Bunker Hill* on 19 February 1945. VF-84 and VMFs -221 and -451 all shared the same aircraft while aboard the carrier. Following the *Bunker Hill*'s retirement, many of the Corsairs went to Okinawa, where some were used by VMF-323 (*National Archives*)

beginning of the this campaign the enemy increased their suicide attacks. On 11 May *Bunker Hill* was hit and her three squadrons were put out of the war. Roger Hedrick was aboard the carrier at the time.

Twelve months earlier, Hedrick and VF-17 had been relieved in the Solomons by VF-34 on 7 March 1944, the former having personally accounted for the destruction of nine enemy aircraft during some 250 hours of combat flying. His next tour was aboard *Bunker Hill*, were he served as CO of VF-84. His first credit with the unit occurred on 17 February 1945 when he damaged a *Tony* over the Nakajima factory at Mushashino, in Japan. Hedrick gained his last victories on the 25th of that month when he destroyed two *Frank*s and a Zeke during attacks in the Katori airfield area, bringing his total official credits to 12 confirmed victories and four damaged. Hedrick takes up the story.

'Air Group 84 was equipped with the F4U-1D with which we were very satisfied. "Fighting 84", together with the two Marine squadrons, VMFs -451 and -221, had a total of 72 Corsairs. The had Marines had 18 planes each and we had 36, all tasked with countering the *kamikazes*. There was no new or very different tactic devised when they started throwing their hundreds of planes at us. The fleet would be surrounded by picket destroyers 100 miles from the main Task Group. They took a lot of damage, even though we were doing our best to protect them. It was an almost impossible task because our radars weren't effective.

'On one of our early fighter sweeps over a Japanese airfield my Corsair was hit by ground fire. The only way I could control the aeroplane was by flying with two hands on my stick the whole time. I found later that a control cable and my prop control had been kinked and I couldn't reduce my blade speed. I then encountered and shot down two *Frank*s, finding that they exploded in the same way as the Zero. If fact one of them exploded right in front of me and I flew right through the fireball. I was hunched down, wondering where its damned engine was as I went through the ball of fire. My last kill came shortly after. I caught another Zero and after I'd fired on him, he was going down and I passed right over him. I looked right down into the cockpit as I wasn't more than 20 ft away from him. I don't know why he didn't bail out – he must have been injured or something. After all our hassles we were getting low on fuel, and I was charging on ahead due to the damage to my controls. I had to let go of the stick and with both hands I yanked back the throttle. The tube that contained the cable had been bent, but I managed to get the wire past it and got down to a

78

lower prop setting. At a lower speed I was able to make it back, where they found nine holes in the plane. Those were the last three kills I got. The whole time I was there I never got to fire my guns at anything else.

'The only way to counter the *kamikazes* was to put lots of CAPs up, the best we could provide. At night it was the closest I ever came to claustrophobia. We had VF(N)-76 and their handful of F6F-3N nightfighters aboard, and their sole job was to take care of Japanese nocturnal attacks. We daylight-only pilots would be buttoned up down below the hanger deck in the wardroom playing cards, or reading, when we'd hear the five-inch guns start up and we knew there was a

run coming in. So everybody is puffing like mad on their cigarettes and the room would soon be full of thick smoke. Then the 40 mm opened up and you knew they were getting close, followed by the 20 mm and .50s, by which time we were just holding on, wondering where the damned thing was going to hit. As far as I was concerned there was nothing worse than being buttoned up like that. The *kamikazes* were pretty effective, and I believe they sank 38 ships, with some carriers being hit repeatedly.

'On 11 May we were finally hit aboard *Bunker Hill*. I had led a pre-dawn strike on Okinawan airfields in my role as air group commander, with the sole intent of having a crack at some of these guys before they had the chance to hit us. Adm Mitcher was aboard our carrier as we were his flagship, and after every flight I would go up and report to him for a debrief. He ordered us to restrict ourselves to defence as far as aerial combat was concerned. Flying over Okinawa we operated exclusively in certain areas at pre-determined altitudes in order to avoid tangling with our own defences on the ground, but they were getting clobbered day and night and our avoidance tactics seemingly made no difference – the Marines on the ground started shooting at us as soon as I lead the strike in. We halted our attack, made a large circuit around our target, and waited until it had lightened up so that our guys could see who we were.

'Following the strike we got back aboard the ship at 0900. The vessel was at general quarters, and they had movies playing – it went to "Condition One Easy" at 1000, and I went down to my office which was just below the hangar deck, near the ready room. I had made a change to the torpedo squadron's schedule for that day, and I told the skipper that he could leave his general quarters station. We had just started to discuss the change in the schedule when we felt the impact of the first *kamikaze*. It landed, plane and bomb, whilst our next flight was getting ready to launch. The bomb landed a short distance from the F4U flown by VF-84's CO, Ted Hill. It took out just about all the planes on the flightdeck.

'Less than three minutes later a second *kamikaze* came in, hitting at the

Task Force 58 heading towards Japan in March 1945. In the foreground are F4U-1Ds of Air Group 84, parked on the forward deck of *Bunker Hill*. At that time the Air Group was made up of five squadrons, three Navy and two Marine, with a total of 71 Corsairs (*via Phil Jarrett*)

***Bunker Hill* burns following a *kamikaze* hit on 11 May 1945. Many of her planes were destroyed on the flightdeck whilst preparing to launch a strike. Marine Corsairs in the air at the time of the attack had to land on other carriers (*Robbins Collection*)**

An F4U-1A aboard USS *Franklin*. In March 1945 this carrier boasted three Corsair squadrons – VF-5 and VMFs -214 and -452. Lt(jg) James E Schiller of VF-5 became an ace on 18 March by downing a Zeke, adding to his previous four kills gained in F6Fs. The next day *Franklin* and her Corsairs were put out of the war by a conventional bombing attack (*National Archives*)

Ens Alfred Lerch of VF-10 accounted for six *Nates* and a *Val* northwest of Okinawa on 16 April 1945. On that day his unit destroyed 33 *kamikazes*, and their escorts, heading for US picket destroyers. Other aces involved in this action were Lt Cdr Walter E Clarke, who accounted for three, Lt(jg) Charles D Farmer (4), Lt(jg) Philip L Kirkwood (6), Ens Horace W Heath (3) and Ens Norwald R Quiel (4) (*National Archives via Grant Race*)

junction between the island and the flightdeck. His bomb went off, opening up the deck and killing most of the guys in the ready room. Ted later told me that the flightdeck just folded right up over him. The first thing I did after the initial hit was to grab my recent poker winnings, saying "If I go swimming, this damned money's going with me!" We got out in the passageway. A replenishment group had come in the day before and the place was stacked with crates up to the wardroom. I grabbed some oranges and put two or three in my pockets – we headed through the smoke caused by burning gasoline going down through several levels from the deck above. People were trapped in compartments and so forth. We arrived at the fo'c'stle and I remember a British Navy pilot who was on board as an observer, and with whom I had had discussions about our air operations, fighting the fires alongside us. I have difficulty with the English accent, but I remember him shouting "Get us some more f...ing hose down here!"

'We got the fires under control at about 1800, and soon after we finally managed to get to the engineering crew, who had been passing out like rats in the engine room due to the terrific heat and smoke – despite this hardship, the ship never went below 10 kts. We then set about trying to get the vessel back up to full speed as the Japs would be all over us due to the horrible pall of smoke we were putting up, advertising where we were. Somewhere along the way I ran into our Chief Engineer and he was in shock, wandering around just like a zombie. All I could think to do was hand him these oranges I'd picked up a while before. He had done such a marvellous job keeping *Bunker Hill* mobile. It wasn't till the next morning that all the fires were finally put out. From the wardroom I came up to the hanger deck, totally forgetting that that was where all my unit's casualties were laid out – the image that greeted me will stay etched in my mind forever. We buried them at sea the next day. The *kamikaze* strikes put an end to our combat tour.'

MARINE F4Us on Okinawa

Marine Corsairs arrived on Okinawa on 7 April in the form of MAG-31 – similarly equipped MAG-33 arrived two days later. Capt Perry Lin Shuman's (6 kills) VMF-311 of MAG-31 were equipped with F4U-1Cs, and operating from Yontan, they gained a total of 71 kills during the campaign. Even more successful was Maj George C Axtell's (6 kills) VMF-323 'Death Rattlers' of MAG-33 who, whilst flying from Kadena, amassed the highest kill tally by claiming 124.5 planes destroyed for no loss to themselves, producing seven aces in the process.

This unit was the last USMC Corsair squadron formed during World War 2. They flew ground attack missions against targets on Okinawa and Japan, as well as tackling *kamikazes*. In the following interviews, three of the unit's pilots, George Axtell (the unit's first CO), Jerry O'Keefe (7 kills) and Jack Broering describe some of VMF-323's operations.

George Axtell – 'I was a flight instructor at Cherry Point in 1943, conducting instrument training in SNJs. I was a junior Major whilst my commanding officer in charge of MAG-32 was Guadalcanal Medal of Honor winner Lt Col John L Smith (19 kills on F4Fs). We flew together and became close friends. At that time Marine aviation was expanding rapidly, and although young and believing myself to be unqualified, Smith gave me command of VMF-323. I took it on and decided that the group I had was going to be the best. We didn't know what the hell we were doing, but we thought we could whip everybody else. We had no doubts in our abilities and confidently took on Guadalcanal veterans during our combat training. We also did intercepts on Army Air Force B-24s and B-25s, making regular attacks on them. I told my men that when they made vertical runs all they had to do was keep their pipper on the nose of the bomber, and they would then pass right by its tail and miss the bomber behind. We also made runs from the low front quarter, coming in to their noses, then rolling over and down. The first time we did this I rolled over and dived to attack first, followed by my unit. The bombers scattered all over, as they must have been green pilots. They didn't want us to fly any more intercepts against them!

'Most of our kills were "flamers" – a big red fire ball. The aircraft on fire would normally blow up, usually just as you went past him. We had gun cameras, but unfortunately they weren't the best, and we had a hard time seeing exactly what we had caught on film. Furthermore, Intelligence took most of them away from us, so we could only use what little we were left with. I wished at the time that we could get copies of them, as we could have learned a lot more, and would therefore had been able to further improve our tactics. A pilot would describe what they saw, but their accounts would often differ from what showed up on the film. The pilot might for instance say that he was about 100 yards behind an enemy aircraft when the film would demonstrate that he was at least 300 yards away. The film also enabled us to co-ordinate times and positions, and by comparing them we could also verify victory credits.'

Jerry O'Keefe – 'We were sent to the South Pacific after several weeks in Hawaii, doing little to affect the war effort until we arrived at Okinawa during Easter 1945. I was then 21 years old and I believe our CO, Maj Axtell, was either 23 or 24 years old. I believe I was one of the youngest aces at age 21. Axtell, our XO, Jefferson D Dorroh (6 kills), and I all became aces on one flight. Dorroh got six, and Axtell and I five each. This was the first time the three of us had ever encountered the enemy in aerial combat – the date was 22 April 1945.

'On 28 April Axtell was leading a 16-plane flight and I was his section leader, which was my normal place. I spotted "bogies" at three o'clock, well below us and headed south toward the ships at Okinawa. Apparently no-one else in our flight saw the "bogies", so I asked permission to have the formation with my wingman, Lt Bill Hood (5.5 kills). As we turned

F4U-1D Corsairs of VMF-323 head back to base following a ground attack mission on Okinawa. The second aircraft still has two of its 5-in rockets left on the racks. Corsairs based on Kadena and Yontan flew both close air support missions for the ground troops and Combat Air Patrols, defending primarily against *kamikazes*. It was the Corsair's close air support at this time that earned it the appellation 'The Sweetheart of Okinawa' (*USMC via Pete Mersky*)

Maj George C Axtell, Jr, was the youngest CO of a Marine fighter unit when he took command of VMF-323 in 1943. During April 1945 he was credited with the destruction of six Japanese aircraft – on the 22nd he destroyed five *Vals*, damaging three more, and on the 28th he destroyed a *Nate*. Following a ground attack mission he would always unnerve his wingman by flying very low over the target to assess the damage so he could give his commander an accurate report of their mission (*Axtell Collection*)

to our right and began a shallow dive, it became clear that these were "bandits", instead of merely "bogies". I relayed this info back to our flight, which was then to our rear. With hand signals, Hood and I separated, Hood to the right and rear of the "Bandits" and me to the left, rear and also above. The enemy apparently never saw us until we began shooting. Hood got two on his first pass and I got one. I then turned and followed another as he dove straight down, destroying my second enemy. I never saw any enemy planes in flight again. The second action gave me seven victories, and for a time I was the leading ace on Okinawa. Later, Lts J W Ruhsam and R Wade each scored seven kills. as well'

Jack Broering – 'The frontline was only six miles away from the field on Okinawa so we could see other Corsairs making their runs. We were also close enough to take ground fire but, as the campaign progressed, we got further and further out of their range.

'Bombing and rocket attacks were quite similar, differing in only by the amount of lead you give the target. Our rockets – 3¹/2 and 5 in rounds – were fine weapons. I liked them as I thought they were the most effective weapons we had. We usually fired them whilst in a 45° dive, making about 400 mph. If you went too fast you'd start losing the covering on the elevator. You could put your "pipper" on the target with rockets, whereas with bombs you had to judge the correct lead so that it landed where you wanted it to. With Napalm we'd make a flatter approach, trying to spread it over a large area. We dropped at about 100 ft, Napalm being contained in our fuel tanks – they weren't too accurate. We used it to effect against tunnels and caves, sometimes managing to put it right into the entrances.

'All of us were trained as fighter pilots, and the ultimate was to go out and shoot somebody down. So we all hoped for that opportunity, but it was a matter of being in the right place at the right time. On 22 April our squadron shot down 25 planes in about 20 minutes. My flight was returning from a routine CAP when they started calling out all the bogies. We had quite a bit of fuel left, but the command ship wouldn't let us return and join the fight as schedules had to be followed. Another time we were on our way out onto station when I spotted four *Tony*s coming by us at a lower altitude. I kept calling them out, but my section leader couldn't see them and wouldn't turn the lead over to me. Other members of my flight also saw them and we were all screaming over the radio and jumping up and down in our cockpits, but to no avail. I couldn't assume the lead, nor leave my position so we had to go sailing on by. It would have been a perfect opportunity for me to gain a victory, but it wasn't to be.

'Fortunately a flight behind us picked them up. On 28 May after a pre-dawn take off we were patrolling our station when the controlling ship kept calling out a bogey. It remained in the same relative position to us all the time and it became apparent that an aircraft was shadowing us in the cloud layer above us. We broke up; two of us going above the clouds while the other two waited below. The enemy must have thought the whole flight was coming up so he went down below. The other section called out that he was down there so we went down too. A path of early morning sunlight was hitting the water and the enemy aircraft was flying right down it – he couldn't get out of it. The other two were waiting for him and they shot down the *Tojo*.'

1st Lt Joseph V Dillard of VMF-323 was credited with 6.333 enemy aircraft, and he is seen here with F4U-1D 'No 51'. His victims were a mixed bag of types, including *Val*s, *Dinah*s, a *Kate* and a *Judy* (*National Archives*)

2nd Lt Robert Wade of VMF-323 again seen in F4U-1D 'No 51'. Although aircraft were not assigned to individual pilots within the unit, this machine does appear to wear Wade's first two kill marks. By the time this picture was taken he had shot down two *Tony*s on 15 April and two *Nate*s and two *Val*s on 4 May. He went on to claim two half-shares in the destruction of both a *Dinah* and a *Val*, as well as damaging three *Nate*s, thus bringing his final score to seven confirmed victories (*National Archives*)

Following *Bunker Hill*'s retirement, *Essex* and *Bennington*'s F4Us would only be accompanied by *Shangri-La* with Air Group 85 aboard. Lt Joe D Robbins (5 kills) was assigned to VBF-8 which flew the F4U-1C. He had previously gained two victories flying the F6F with VF-6 aboard *Intrepid*.

'On 8 April 1945, we departed Ford Island and on 26 April 1945 we joined the carrier Task Force off Okinawa. We had 16 carriers making up three task groups. One Task Group would replenish each day whilst the other two would be hitting targets in Japan. On 4 May I was the flight leader for 12 F4U-1Cs flying CAP over a destroyer 12 miles north of Okinawa. The Japs were sending planes from Japan to attack our forces on Okinawa and ships at sea. At times *kamikaze* planes would be at a low altitude with fighter cover at a higher altitude. Our mission was to intercept and shoot down these aircraft. We launched in the early morning from the *Shangri-La* and took up our station. As always, we charged and test-fired our guns after take-off. My division was assigned an altitude of 20,000 ft, whilst the second division was at 10,000 ft and the third 5000 ft. We had been on station a short time when at 0830 we received a vector at distance 26 miles to a bogey, and we were told that it was below us. I had fuel in the belly tank and I didn't want to drop it until I saw the bogey.

'These flights were about four hours long so you didn't want to drop the tank until you had to. I had my left hand on the switch in preparation, ready to go to the main gas tank and drop the belly store when I saw the bogey. We were all looking down when all of a sudden about 30 Zekes came from above and attacked us. We didn't see them approach as it was hazy and we had also been told they were below us. I switched tanks and dropped the belly tank and made a sharp turn all at the same time – I had to. By doing this, however the engine was not getting any fuel, so it stopped. It takes only a few seconds to switch and get suction again, but I didn't have that few seconds. You don't get suction when you are making sharp turns and I was really making them. One plane was in my gun sight coming from the 10 o'clock position. I tried a 30° deflection shot and pulled the trigger; no guns. I was banking right and then left as steep as I could to keep them from shooting at me, still no engine. I kept recharging the guns and still they wouldn't fire. I kept banking one side and then

to the other, keeping my nose down and losing altitude. I had at least four of them in my sights, but my guns wouldn't fire!

'These enemy planes were escort cover for some *kamikaze* planes below. Although I wasn't hit, they shot down my wingman, Frank Siddall, and second section leader, Sonny Chernoff, and then they left. The division at 5000 ft then intercepted them. I was at about 16,000 ft when I got my engine started, and I followed my wingman down and he made a good landing in the

'No 51' of was obviously a popular aircraft to be photographed with as here its is again, this time with 1st Lt John W Ruhsam posing on its wing. This pilot's final tally was seven confirmed victories and three damaged. Both Ruhsam and Wade flew together and shared their combat victories (*National Archives*)

VMF-323 pilots pose together on the wing of an F4U-1D, with all bar one of them being an ace. From left to right, CO, Maj George C Axtell, Jr (6 victories), XO, Maj Jefferson D Dorroh (6 victories), 1st Lt Normand T Theriault (2.25 victories), 1st Lt Albert P Wells (5 victories), 1st Lt Francis A Terrill (6.083 victories), 2nd Lt Charles W Drake (5 victories), 1st Lt Joseph V Dillard (6.333 victories), 1st Lt Jeremiah J O'Keefe (7 victories), 2nd Lt Dewey F Durnford (6.333 victories) and 1st Lt William L Hood, Jr (5.5 victories) (*Axtell Collection*)

water. I stayed over him until a destroyer picked him up 35 minutes later. The destroyer that rescued him, the *St George*, was hit by a *kamikaze* two days later while he was still aboard.

'Out of the four planes in my division, none of the guns would fire. At that time we were the only Navy unit that had the 20 mm guns. That afternoon they were tested at high altitude and it was found that they froze and would not fire at about 15,000 ft. We checked with Washington and learned that the flights that were to test them at high altitude had been cancelled! From then on we were restricted to 12,000 ft until we got gun heaters. We still flew CAPs and target strikes below this altitude. VBF-85 (.50 cal) flew the higher CAPs.

'On 11 May 1945 I was on another early morning take-off to fly target CAP over our destroyer, again about 12 miles north of Okinawa. We had 16 F4U-1Cs up, and this time because of the gun freezing problems, my two divisions were at a lower altitude – 6000 ft – whilst our XO, Lt Cdr Hubert, was the mission leader flying with two divisions at 12,000 ft. Again my wingman was Frank Siddall. After about an hour on station, we were given a vector to the north. We flew for about five minutes (25 miles) and then sighted about 16 Zekes directly ahead and a little below. They were in no particular formation – Zekes just tended to fly together. My altitude was about 5000 ft when they were sighted – they were at about 4000 ft. I was leading the two divisions and the second division was on my starboard side.

'I spotted them first and made a left turn. During the turn I broke off to make a run on them, and as I started down, they just broke up going in all directions. The rest of the formation followed me down, each picking out a plane. I picked out one on the outside of my dive. He just took off heading west and dove down to about 1000 ft. I was on his tail and there were others going in the same direction. This is not the desired type of attack, but we had to get them quickly before they got to our ships. We couldn't make runs on them and pull up because there wasn't enough time. A Zeke and I were going about the same speed. I was in range, about 600 ft behind him, so I opened fire with no deflection. I aimed at the middle of his fuselage. Firing one medium burst, I saw the bullets hit the aircraft, every third bullet being an explosive. I could see damage to his tail, but no fire. He rolled over into a "Split S" and went down, and that's the last I saw of him. It all happened so fast I couldn't tell if I hit the pilot. Since I was firing 20 mm they should have gotten through to him. I don't

1st Lt Jeremiah J O'Keefe of VMF-323 indicates his final tally of seven victories whilst in the cockpit of F4U-1D 'No 26'. On 22 April, during a 20-minute engagement, VMF-323 pilots destroyed 24.75 aircraft, O'Keefe downing five *Vals*, one of which attempted to ram his F4U before hitting the sea (*O'Keefe Collection*)

F4U-1D 'No 31' of VMF-323 undergoes maintenance on Okinawa in late April 1945. This aircraft was one of the machines flown by 1st Lt Francis A Terrill, and it appears rather worn with its underside splattered with mud (*Broering Collection*)

think there was any way he could have survived, but I didn't claim a kill because I didn't see him crash or burn – he was listed as damaged.

'I looked left and there was the second Zeke. He just came over and parked in front of me as they were split up and flying all over the area. I had made a slight left turn and he had probably been trying to make a run on us and ended up there. He was about 750 ft away and within range so I fired a medium burst. He

caught fire and the gun camera film later showed a parachute. Except for the fire, I saw no damage to the plane. Again I looked left and there was a third Zeke. I didn't think all of the planes were *kamikazes* because they were trying to attack me – *kamikazes* carried bombs but no guns or parachutes. Some probably were *kamikazes*, but from above I did not see any bombs. I would rather have got the *kamikazes* if I could tell which ones they were, since they were the ones that went after our ships.

'The third Zeke was at 10 o'clock but out of range (about 2000 ft away) at about the same altitude as I was (1000 feet). I turned left about 20 ° and started chasing him. We chased him for about 10 miles when we came to the island of Tari Shima. He got down to about 100 ft off the water and close to the island. I didn't tell my wingman, Frank Siddall, to keep on his tail – I didn't have to. He saw what I was doing, and that this way one of us would get him. He had been my wingman for a long time, and a good one. He was always there with me, and most of the time I didn't have to tell him what to do. We had the Zeke boxed in, and if he didn't go around the island then Frank would be on his tail. The island wasn't very high, reaching 300 ft in places over its two-mile length.

'I assumed the Zeke was going around the island because he made a 30° left turn. He was very close to the island and low, at about 100 ft. He had started a left turn at the other end of the island. The only chance he had was to try to trick us into following him around low. You didn't make tight turns in the F4U at low altitude as it would stall and spin. The Zeke could out-turn us and gain distance, then try to pull away from us and go home. I pulled up making a left turn, then a right and got him on a head-on. He was about 800 ft ahead of and slightly below me when I fired. This makes an easy shot because you can aim ahead of him; he would run into the bullets, without deflection, just a high-to-low head-on shot. I gave it a long burst. I didn't see the bullets strike. I just pulled the trigger and he blew to hell – a big ball of fire. I took a south-east heading in the direction of our station.

'It was only a couple of minutes before I saw a fourth Zeke – he could have been coming to help the one I just shot down. He was at my eleven o'clock position. He had been heading toward me, but made a left turn and took up a course about the same as mine. I was at about 500 ft and he was lower. He dove even lower to pick up speed, getting down to between 10 to 25 ft above the water. I was then at about 100 ft, with my wingman on my right wing. I was wide open for at least ten minutes and wasn't gaining on him. After we landed, my wingman told me that at the time sparks were coming out of my exhaust. The F4U top speed was 405 mph at sea level, so the Zeke was also moving at about that speed. I was probably gaining a little on him, but I couldn't stay wide open much longer or I would burn up my engine. If I fixed my sights on him in level position my bullets would hit the water behind him. By raising my nose the bullets would go

Capt Kenneth A Walsh pictured in his F4U-4 'No 13', BuNo 80879, following his 21st kill on 22 June 1945. On this day he shot down a *kamikaze* over northern Okinawa whilst serving with VMF-222. Minutes after this picture was taken, his crewchief, Sgt Harry Ross (seen left), attached the final kill decal. The F4U-4 was the most advanced variant of the Corsair to see service during World War 2, its primary differences compared with previous models being a larger engine, four bladed prop, revised air ducts (resulting in the characteristic cowling chin), a revised cockpit, including a raised deck, armoured seat, better instrument layout and an improved bubble canopy (*Walsh Collection*)

The USS *Shangri-La* on 17 August 1945. Her Air Group 85 Corsairs have the new single letter 'Z' marking that was adopted on 27 July to replace the short-lived 'G' symbol system (a white lightning bolt) (*Robbins Collection*)

85

straight for about 800-900 ft, then drop downward due to gravity. Even if he was 800 ft away, I would have to raise my sights above him. When I fired, he was at the right distance, but by the time the bullets got there he had moved. Like a deflection shot, you have to aim at the point the plane will be when the bullets get there. I knew I couldn't continue wide open for much longer. I was gaining on him too slowly.

'My job was to shoot him down and I didn't want to be the one to have to land in the water. I had used up a lot of ammo already and I wasn't going to waste any – there could be several more out there we could run into. My plan was to try to lob the bullets into him so I fired another short burst. He hit the water and bounced back up and kept going. I knew I had the right angle on raising my nose so I fired again. He hit the water again and bounced back up. Again I fired and he hit the water and came back up. The fourth time he went down to stay. The gun camera showed all of this on film – the parachute of No 2, No 3 blowing up and No 4 bouncing off the water. The camera had a few seconds override so it showed things the pilot didn't see. After number four it had been a long day, and I was tired. We reported to our control ship and the two of us returned to the carrier.

'On 10 July 1945, I was part of a 16-plane fighter sweep over airfields in the Tokyo area. Our mission was to knock out the Japanese Air Force, either on the ground or in the air. Sweeps were made on Katori, Choisi, Konoiki, Ikisu, Kitaura, Hokoda, Kashiwa, Imba and Shiroi airfields. It was a successful day, with considerable damage being done to Jap aircraft on the ground. No airborne enemy opposition was encountered. From 10 July to 15 August we continued to fly sweeps on Japan, which mostly consisted of targets of opportunity in Hokaido, Tokyo, Honshu, Kyushu and Osaka. Our weaponry was usually made up four 20 mm cannon, eight 8-inch rockets and either a single 1000- or two 500-lb bombs. Each flight over Japan we would hit several targets, diving in from about 20,000 ft. In each dive we would first shoot the four 20 mm cannon, then fire a couple of 8-inch rockets and then drop a bomb.

'On 15 August 1945 at 0530 we took off with a flight of 12 planes to hit the Tokyo Shibura electric plant with a dozen 1000-lb bombs. This site was a priority target, having never been hit before. Just as we got to within sight of the coast of Japan the recall was given. "Jettison bombs and returns to base; the War is over." We dropped our ordnance in the water and headed back. It was cloudy and some people were up above the clouds and I heard people screaming "Don't drop now, we're below you!"

'We ceased offensive operations and were merely told to protect our-selves by "shooting down snoopers", not vindictively, but in a "friendly" way! Japanese planes did continue their attacks in considerable num-ber, numerous planes were shot down, mostly by anti-aircraft fire and RAPCAPS (Patrol Fighters sta-tioned about 20-30 miles from the fleet). On 22 August 22 I flew in a 1000-plane dress formation over the fleet to mark the end of the war.'

Lt Joe D Robbins pictured on the wing of one of VF-85's F4U-1Ds. These aircraft were soon replaced with new F4U-1Cs to serve in the fighter role, whilst VBF-85 retained their Ds for ground attack duties. Having previously flown the F6F Hellcat, Robbins thought the F4U was easier to land on board the carrier due to the better bubble canopy incorporated on the later marks (*Robbins Collection*)

On 24 July 1945 Robbins, flying F4U-1C BuNo 82749, performed a *Dumbo* escort to the Inland Sea, near Kobe. The 'X' in this shot shows the location of a downed *Yorktown* pilot, and above to the right can be seen an F6F-P. A little higher towards the centre of the picture is an F4U – both aircraft were part of the rescue effort. Whilst the flying boat landed and successfully picked up the pilot, Robbins and other members of Air Group 85 strafed gun positions firing from all around. During this mission VF-85 pilot Lt(jg) R A Bloomfield shot down an *Oscar*, whilst three VBF-85 pilots shared the credit for damag-ing another (*Robbins Collection*)

THE APPENDICES

Corsair Squadrons in which aces served

USMC

VMFs -112, -113, -121, -122, -124, -211, -212, -213, -214, -215, -221, -222, -223, -311, -312, -321, -322, -323, -351 and -451

USN

VFs -5, -10, -17, -84, -85 and VBF-83

FAA

No 47 NW and No 1836 Sqn

ACES' CORSAIR CARRIER DEPLOYMENTS

HMS Victorious
No 1836 Sqn (July 1944-August 1945) – Sheppard
No 47 FW (July 1944-August 1945) – Hay

USS Essex (CV-9)
VMF-124 (January-March 1945) – Finn
VMF-213 (January-March 1945) – Thomas
VBF-83 (March-August 1945) – Godson, W H Harris, Kincaid and Reidy

USS Intrepid (CV-11)
VF-10 (March-August 1945) – Clarke, Farmer, Gray, Heath, Kirkwood, Lerch and Quiel

USS Franklin (CV-13)
VF-5 (February-March 1945) – Schiller

USS Bunker Hill (CV-17)
VF-84 (January-June 1945) – Chambers, Freeman, Gildea, Hedrick, Laney Marchant, Sargent and Smith
VMF-221 (February-May 1945) – Snider, Balch, Baldwin and Swett
VMF-451 (February-May 1945) – Long and Donnahue

USS Bennington (CV-20)
VMF-112 (January-June 1945) Hansen and Owen

USS Shangri-La (CV-38)
VF-85 (May-August 1945) – Robbins

USS Cape Gloucester (CVE-109)
VMF-351 (April-August 1945) – Yost

CORSAIR ACES

This comprehensive list covers only aerial victories that were officially credited. Included are aces that gained kills in other types as well as the F4U. The unit entries give the squadron in which a pilot scored the majority of his F4U kills. Credits are listed as Destroyed/Probable/Damaged, whilst the figure in brackets gives the pilot's F4U kills if he scored victories in other fighters as well. In total the aces scored 545.25 kills in the South West Pacific, compared to 240.083 in the Central Pacific.

Name	Rank	Service	Unit	Kills (F4U)
Aldrich, D N	Capt	USMC	VMF-215;	20/6/0
Alley, Jr, S C	2nd Lt	USMC	VMF-323	5/0/0
Axtell, Jr G C	Maj	USMC	VMF-323	6/0/3
Balch, D L	Capt	USMC	VMF-221	5/1/2
Baldwin, F B	Capt	USMC	VMF-221	5/1/12.5
Blackburn, J T	Lt Cdr	USN	VF-17	11/5/3
Bolt, Jnr, J F	1st Lt	USMC	VMF-214	6/0/0
Boyington, G	Maj	USMC	VMF-214	28/4/0 (22)
Braun, R L	Capt	USMC	VMF-215	5/2/1
Brown, Jr, W P	2nd Lt	USMC	VMF-311	7/0/0
Burris, H M	Lt(jg)	USN	VF-17	7.5/0/0
Carl, M E	Maj	USMC	VMF-223	18.5/0/3 (2)
Carlton, W A	Capt	USMC	VMF-212	5/2/1
Case, W N	1st Lt	USMC	VMF-214	8/1/0
Caswell, D	2nd Lt	USMC	VMF-221	7/1/0
Chambers, C J	Lt(jg)	USN	VF-84	5.333/0/1
Chandler, C	1st Lt	USMC	VMF-215	6/0/0
Chenoweth, O I	Lt	USN	VF-17	8.5/2/0 (7.5)

Name	Rank	Service	Unit	Kills (F4U)
Clarke, W E	Lt Cdr	USN	VF-10	7/0/0 (3)
Conant, A R	Capt	USMC	VMF-215	6/3/0
Cordray, P	Lt	USN	VF-17/-10	7/1/3
Crowe, W E	Capt	USMC	VMF-124	7/1/1
Cunningham, D G	Lt(jg)	USN	VF-17	7/0/1.25
Cupp, J N	Capt	USMC	VMF-213	12.5/2/0
Davenport, M W	Lt	USN	VF-17	6.25/0/0
DeLong, P C	1st Lt	USMC	VMF-212	11.166/1/2
Dillard, J V	1st Lt	USMC	VMF-323	6.333/0/0
Dillow, E	1st Lt	USMC	VMF-221	6/2/1
Donahue, A G	Maj	USMC	VMF-112	14/1/0 (12)
Dorroh, J D	Maj	USMC	VMF-323	6/2/0
Drake, C W	2nd Lt	USMC	VMF-323	5/1/0
Durnford, D F	2nd Lt	USMC	VMF-323	6.333/0/0
Elwood, H McJ	Maj	USMC	VMF-212	5.166/2/0
Everton, L D	Maj	USMC	VMF-113	12/1/0 (2)
Farmer, C D	Lt(jg)	USN	VF-10	7.25/0/0 (4)
Farrel, W	1st Lt	USMC	VMF-312	5/1/0
Finn, H J	Capt	USMC	VMF-124	6/0/05
Fisher, D E	1st Lt	USMC	VMF-214	6/1/0
Ford, K M	Capt	USMC	VMF-121	5/1/0
Freeman, D C	Lt	USN	VF-17/-84	9/2/0
Gildea, J T	Lt(jg)	USN	VF-84	7/1/2
Gile, C D	Lt	USN	VF-17	8/0/05
Godson, L W	Lt	USN	VBF-83	5/0/0
Gray, L E	Lt(jg)	USN	VF-10	5.25/0/0 (2)

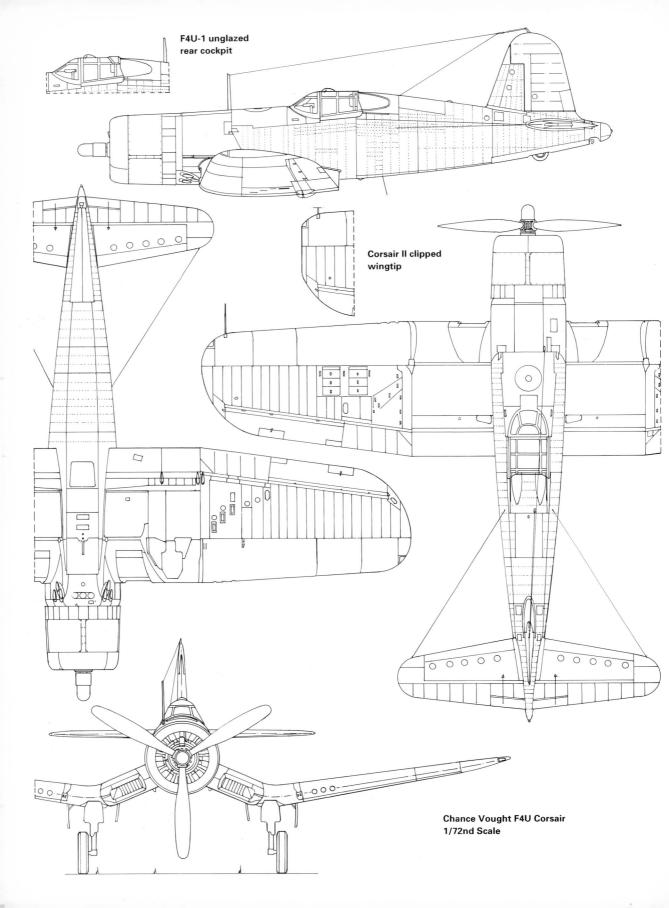

F4U-1 unglazed
rear cockpit

Corsair II clipped
wingtip

Chance Vought F4U Corsair
1/72nd Scale

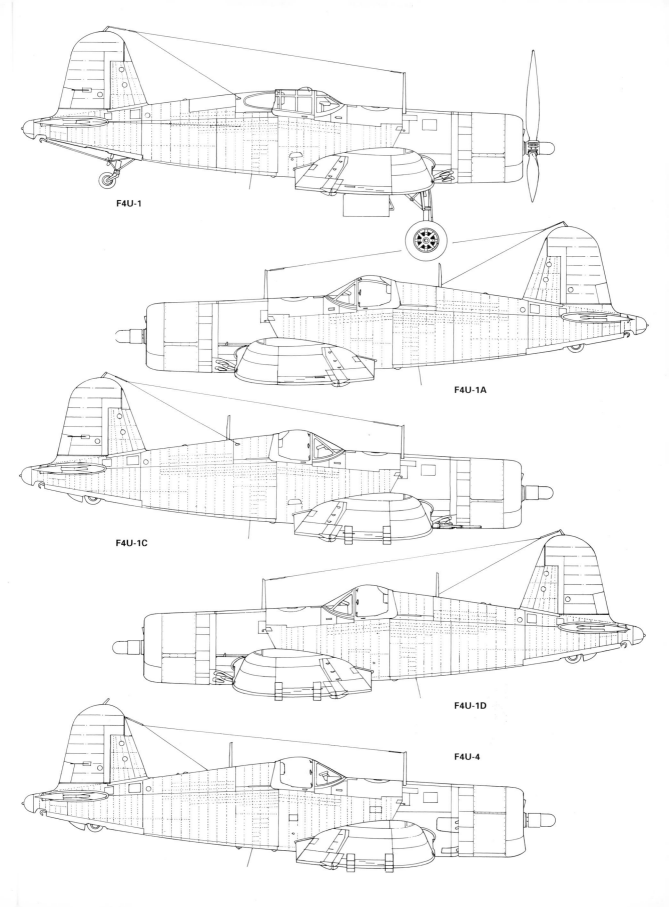

F4U-1

F4U-1A

F4U-1C

F4U-1D

F4U-4

Name	Rank	Service	Unit	Kills (F4U)
Gutt, F E	Capt	USMC	VMF-223	8/0/1(4)
Hacking, Jr, A E	1st Lt	USMC	VMF-221	5/0/0
Hall, S O	1st Lt	USMC	VMF-213	6/0/0
Hansen, Jr, H	Maj	USMC	VMF-112	5.5/0/2.5
Hanson, R M	1st Lt	USMC	VMF-215/-214	25/2/0
Harris, W H	Lt	USN	VBF-83	5/0/1
Hay, R C	Lt Col	RM	No 47 NW	7/0/3 (4)
Heath, H W	Ens	USN	VF-10	7/0/0
Hedrick, R R	Lt Cdr	USN	VF-17/-84	12/0/4
Hernan, Jr, E J	1st Lt	USMC	VMF-215	8/1/0
Hood, Jr, W L 1st	Lt	USMC	VMF-323	5.5/0/2
Hundley, J C	1st Lt	USMC	VMF-211	6/1/0
Ireland, J W	Maj	USMC	VMF-211	5.333/2/0
Jensen, A J	1st Lt	USMC	VMF-214/-441	7/1/0
Jones, C D	2nd Lt	USMC	VMF-222	6/1/1
Kepford, I C	Lt(jg)	USN	VF-17	16/1/1
Kincaid, R A	Lt	USN	VBF-83	5/0/0
Kirkwood, P L	Lt(jg)	USN	VF-10	12/1/0 (8)
Laney, W G	Lt	USN	VF-84	5/2/1
Lerch, A	Ens	USN	VF-10	7/0/0
Long, H H	Maj	USMC	VMF-121/-451	10/0/0 (7)
Lynch, J P	Capt	USMC	VMF-224	5.5/0/0 (2)
Maas, Jr, J B	Maj	USMC	VMF-112/-322	5.5/1/0 (2.5)
Magee, C L	1st Lt	USMC	VMF-214	9/2/0
Maberry, L A	Lt(jg)	USN	VF-84	5/0/0
March, Jr, H A	Lt	USN	VF-17	5/0/0 (4)
May, E	Lt(jg)	USN	VF-17	8.5/0/0
McCartney H A	1st Lt	USMC	VMF-121/-214	5/2.5/0 (4)
McClurg R W	1st Lt	USMC	VMF-214	7/2/0
McManus, J	1st Lt	USMC	VMF-221	6/0/0
Mims, R	Lt(jg)	USN	VF-17	6/3/0
Morgan, J L	1st Lt	USMC	VMF-213	8.5/0/0
Mullen, P A	1st Lt	USMC	VMF-214/-122/-112	6.5/1/1
O'Keefe, J J	1st Lt	USMC	VMF-323	7/0/0
Olander, E L	Capt	USMC	VMF-214	5/4/0
Overend, E F	Maj	USMC	VMF-321	8.333/0/0 (3)
Owen, D C	Capt	USMC	VMF-112	5/0/1 (2.5)
Owens, Jr, R G	Maj	USMC	VMF-215	7/4/0
Percy, J G	1st Lt	USMC	VMF-112	6/0/1 (1)
Pierce, Jr, F E	Capt	USMC	VMF-121	6/1/0 (1)
Pittman Jr, J	2nd Lt	USMC	VMF-221	5/2/0 (3)
Porter, R B	Maj	USMC	VMF-121	5/1/1 (3)
Poske, G 'H'	Maj	USMC	VMF-212	5/1/0
Post, Jr, N T	Maj	USMC	VMF-221	8/0/0 (5)
Powell, E A	Capt	USMC	VMF-122	5/0/0 (4)
Quiel, N R	Ens	USN	VF-10	6/0/0
Reidy, T H	Lt	USN	VBF-83	10/0/0
Reinburg, J H	Maj	USMC	VMF-122	7/2/0 (4)
Robbins, J D	Lt	USN	VF-85	5/0/1 (3)
Ruhsam, J W	1st Lt	USMC	VMF-323	7/0/3
Sapp, D H	Maj	USMC	VMF-222	10/4/2
Sargent, J J	Lt(jg)	USN	VF-84	5.25/0/2 (1)
Scarborough, Jr, H V	1st Lt	USMC	VMF-214	5/0/0
Schiller, J E	Lt(jg)	USN	VF-5	5/1/0 (1)
See, R B	1st Lt	USMC	VMF-321	5/0/0
Segal, H E	1st Lt	USMC	VMF-221	12/1/0
Shaw, E O	1st Lt	USMC	VMF-213	14.5/1/0
Sheppard, D J	Lt	RCNVR	No 1836 Sqn	5/1/0
Shuman, P L	Capt	USMC	VMF-121	5/1/0
Sigler, W E	Capt	USMC	VMF-112/124	5.333/1/0 (4.333)
Smith, J M	Lt(jg)	USN	VF-17/-84	10/3/1
Snider, W N	1st Lt	USMC	VMF-221	11.5/1/0 (8.5)
Spears, H L	Capt	USMC	VMF-215	15/3/0
Streig, F J	Lt(jg)	USN	VF-17	5/0/2
Swett, J E	Capt	USMC	VMF-221	15.5/4/0.25 (8.5)
Synar, S T	1st Lt	USMC	VMF-112	5/0/0 (3)
Terrill, F A	1st Lt	USMC	VMF-323	6.083/0/4
Thomas, Jr, F C	1st Lt	USMC	VMF-211	9/2.5/4
Thomas, W J	Capt	USMC	VMF-213	18.5/3.333/3
Valentine, H J	Capt	USMC	VMF-312	6/1/0
Vedder, M N	1st Lt	USMC	VMF-213	6/0/0 (4)
Wade, R	1st Lt	USMC	VMF-323	7/0/3
Walsh, K A	Capt	USMC	VMF-124/-222	21/2/1
Warner, A T	Maj	USMC	VMF-215	8/2/0 (7)
Weissenberger, G J	Maj	USMC	VMF-213	5/0/0
Wells, A P	1st Lt	USMC	VMF-323	5/0/0
Williams G M H	1st Lt	USMC	VMF-215	7/2/0
Yost, D K	Lt Col	USMC	VMF-351	8/0/0 (2)
Yunck, M R	Maj	USMC	VMF-311	5/0/0 (2)

COLOUR PLATES

1
F4U-1 black 17 of 1st Lt Howard J Finn, VMF-124, Guadalcanal, February 1943

Finn was flying this aircraft on 14 February during the 'St Valentines Day Massacre'. He left formation to chase a lone Zero and was then attacked by more aircraft. He returned to the formation, taking refuge under a B-24, the gunners of which claimed the destruction of one of his pursuers. The next day AAF intelligence officers arrived at his base requesting that the 'pilot of "No 17"' verify the gunners claim. This aircraft has the early style black code under the canopy as it appeared at the start of the unit's combat operations. The two-tone paint scheme consisted of Blue Grey upper surfaces with Light Grey under surfaces, except for the folding portion of the wing where the upper surface colour was also used.

2
F4U-1 white 13/BuNo 02350 of 2nd Lt Kenneth A Walsh, VMF-124, Munda, August 1943

The aircraft wears a revised white 13 forward of the national insignia. The early style black number can still be seen under the canopy and on the cowling. When VMF–124 first received their Corsairs, the CO, Maj Gise, assigned aircraft to each of his pilots, and they were required to work on the Corsair with the crewchiefs in order to familiarise themselves with the F4U-1.

3
F4U-1 white 114 of 2nd Lt Kenneth A Walsh, VMF-124, Munda, August 1943

Walsh destroyed two *Vals* and a Zero in this machine near Vella Lavella on 15 August 1943. Although his log book shows he was flying BuNo

02350, this was an error caused by the confused state of operations during the Vella Lavella campaign. White 114 was a pool aircraft based at Munda, its code not being related to its BuNo.

4
F4U-1 white 13 of 1st Lt Kenneth A Walsh, VMF-124, Russell Islands, September 1943

Walsh flew this aircraft towards the end of his third tour. It has a white 13 aft of the canopy and field-applied bars added to the national insignia. Following his tour Walsh became a Training Command instructor at NAS Jacksonville, before returning to combat in April 1945 with VMF-222.

5
F4U-1 white 7 *DAPHNE C*/BuNo 02350 of Capt James N Cupp, VMF-213, Guadalcanal, July 1943

Cupp claimed his first two kills (a *Betty* and a Zero) in this aircraft on 15 July 1943 during his second tour. The aircraft wears a white 7 in place of the previous number 13 just forward of the national insignia. The old style black 13 is just visible under the canopy and on the cowl. The aircraft bears four kill marks, representing Cupp's next victories claimed on the 17th in F4U-1 BuNo 02580.

6
F4U-1 white 15 *DAPHNE C*/BuNo 03829 of Capt James N Cupp, VMF-213, Munda, September 1943

Cupp claimed two victories (a *Tony* and a Zero) in this aircraft on 11 September 1943, bringing his total claims up to 7 / . The aircraft wears a white 15 and six whole kill marks. The cowling has been taken from F4U-1 white 7/BuNo 02350, and still bears the legend *DAPHNE C*, together with the small white 13.

7
F4U-1 white 11 *Defabe* of 1st Lt George C Defabio, VMF-213, Guadalcanal, July 1943

This was the aircraft that bore Defabio's personal markings, which comprised a pair of dice and the name *Defabe*. Although not an ace, he did claim three Zeros on 30 June and on 11 and 17 July 1943. Although individual aircraft were assigned to pilots within the unit, it was seldom the case that they flew them on their assigned missions. As ops officer, Jim Cupp would allocate pilots any serviceable aircraft available, without reference to numbers and names of the fighters concerned. Defabio did happen to be flying this F4U-1 when hit by flak over Munda in July, however.

8
F4U-1 white 10 *GUS'S GOPHER* of 1st Lt Wilbur J Thomas, VMF-213, Guadalcanal, July 1943

Thomas's 'GOPHER bears eight kill marks below the canopy and a *Disney* character on the cowling. The kill marks represent seven confirmed victories and a probable claimed during his second tour. On 30 June he downed his first four Zeros and one probable over Blanche Channel. His next victories, two Zeros and a *Betty*, were claimed on 15 July near Vella Lavella. Thomas went on to be VMF-213's most successful ace with 18.5 kills, 3.333 probables and 3 damaged. Most were achieved in the South West Pacific theatre during 1943, although he later bagged two Zeros and a 0.333 probable, plus damaged two *Oscars*, in February 1945 during a cruise on the USS *Essex*.

9
F4U-1 white 10 *GUS'S GOPHER* of 1st Lt Wilbur J Thomas, VMF-213, Guadalcanal, July 1943

The starboard side of Thomas's 'GOPHER, showing its name. Virtually all of VMF-213's aircraft were decorated in a similar way, with a name on one side of the cowling and an artwork on the other. All F4U-1s wore white numbers on the fuselage forward of the national insignia, and a smaller black number on the undercarriage door.

10
F4U-1 white 20 of 1st Lt Foy R Garison, VMF-213, Guadalcanal, July 1943

Garison failed to reach the status of ace, but did claim two Zeros on 30 June 1943, before being killed in action on 17 July. His aircraft was adorned with a beautifully painted eagle on the cowling. Like most early F4U-1s, his aircraft was equipped with only the forward antenna mast, which in this case was the shorter of the two types employed.

11
F4U-1 white 125/BuNo 02487 of 2nd Lt Donald L Balch, VMF-221, Guadalcanal, July 1943

This was the F4U flown by Balch on 6 July when he destroyed a Zero near Rendova. He claimed two kills in the Solomons and later brought his total up to five whilst aboard *Bunker Hill* in 1945.

12
F4U-1 white 590/BuNo 17590 of Capt Arthur R Conant, VMF-215 Barakoma/Torokina, January 1944

Conant destroyed a Zero whilst flying this aircraft on an escort mission to Rabaul on 14 January 1944. VMF-215 pilots did not have individual F4Us assigned to them, and rarely flew the same Corsair more than once. Conant's other kills were as follows – two *Tonys* confirmed and two probables on 25 August 1943 whilst flying F4U-1 BuNo 02371, one Zero on 1 September 1943 flying an F4U-1, one Zero on 30 January 1944 flying F4U-1 BuNo 17833, one Zero on 18 January 1944 flying F4U-1A BuNo 17735. F4U-1 white 590/BuNo 17590 lacks the curved glazing aft of the canopy, as well as the glazed canopy rear itself. The national insignia has field-applied bars, and the white aircraft number has been applied over a previous code, utilising the last three digits of the BuNo.

13

F4U-1A white 735/BuNo 17735 of Capt Arthur R Conant, VMF-215 Barakoma/Torokina, January 1944

Conant destroyed a Zero whilst flying this aircraft on an escort to Rabaul on 18 January 1944. F4U-1A BuNo 17735 appears in a very weathered three-tone scheme with field applied bars to its national insignia. This scheme followed the principle of Counter Shading/Counter Shadowing and attempted to counteract the effects of light falling on an aircraft. As light normally comes from above, upper surfaces would be light whilst lower surfaces would be darker. Therefore, darker colours were applied to the upper surfaces, gradually blending to white on the under surfaces. Shaded areas under horizontal surfaces were to be painted white to counteract shadowing. The scheme used semi-gloss Sea Blue on the upper surfaces except where it could cause glare, whereupon it was replaced with nonspecular Sea Blue. Intermediate Blue was used on the fin and Insignia White was employed on the under-surfaces. The fuselage sides were meant to be graded from dark blue to white, but in practice Intermediate Blue was applied. This scheme was authorised on 5 January 1943.

14

F4U-1 white 75 of Maj Robert G Owens, Jr, VMF-215, Munda, August 1943

Owens gained seven confirmed kills and four probables. He destroyed a Zero on 21 August 1943 with BuNo 02656, one Zero and two probables on 22 August, another Zero on 30 August, two Zeros on 14 January 1944 whilst flying BuNo 17927 and another on the 22nd whilst flying BuNo 17937. He claimed a *Tojo* and a Zero probable on 24 January whilst flying F4U-1A BuNo 55825.

15

F4U-1 white 76 *Spirit of '76*/BuNo 02714 of Maj Robert G Owens, Jr, VMF-215 Munda, August 1943

Although Owens authorised this F4U to be called *Spirit of '76*, it was not actually assigned to him, and he only flew it once on a 'local patrol' from Munda on 31 July 1943. It has a field-applied three-tone scheme with the intermediate tone carefully graded to intermediate white. This contrasts with the factory-applied scheme which has a distinct demarcation line between the colours. The national insignia has been updated with the application of white bars and an Insignia Blue surround to the whole design. This style of insignia came into force from 31 July 1943.

16

F4U-1A white 596/BuNo 17596 of 1st Lt Robert M Hanson, VMF-215, Torokina, February 1944

Hanson was one of the most successful US aces of the war, claiming 25 kills and two probables, all of which were gained in the brief period between 4 August 1943 and 30 January 1944. When he encountered the enemy Hanson usually claimed multiple victories – on 14 January 1944 he downed five Zeros, on the 24th he claimed another four, on the 26th three and a probable, and on the 30th two Zeros and two *Tojos*. Hanson was killed by ground fire while attacking gun emplacements near Cape St George, New Ireland, on 3 February 1944.

17

F4U-1A white 777/BuNo 17777 of 1st Lt Phillip C DeLong, VMF-212, Vella Lavella, November 1943

Delong was the highest-scoring F4U ace to serve with VMF-212, being credited with a total of 11.166 confirmed victories, a probable and two damaged. His confirmed kills were as follows – two Zeros and one damaged on 9 January 1944 flying F4U-1A BuNo 17878, two Zeros on 17 January flying F4U-1A BuNo 17485, 1.8333 Zeros on 23 January flying F4U-1A BuNo 17878, one Zero on 29 January flying F4U-1A BuNo 17894, one *Hamp* on 31 January flying F4U-1A BuNo 17879, and three *Vals* on 15 February flying F4U-1A BuNo 55809. He flew white 777 on 4, 12, 13 and 18 November.

18

F4U-1A white 722A/BuNo 17722 of 1st Lt Phillip C DeLong, VMF-212, Vella Lavella, November 1943

DeLong flew this F4U on 11 November whilst providing cover for Task Force 50, striking Rabaul. It wears the three-tone scheme with its number forward of the national insignia. When aircraft utilised the last three digits of the BuNo as an identifying code, occasionally a unit would end up with two machines with the same number. In the event of this occurring the letter 'A' was added to one of the codes, as has happened here.

19

F4U-1 white 576 *MARINE'S DREAM*/BuNo 02576 of 1st Lt Edwin L Olander, VMF-214, Munda, October 1943

Olander shot down a Zero on 17 October 1943 during a sweep to Kahili in this machine. His other kills were one Zero and a probable on 10 October 1943 whilst flying BuNo 02309, one Zero and a probable on 18 October, one Zero on 28 December while flying BuNo 17875 and a Zero and a probable on 30 December whilst flying BuNo 17792. Olander's final score was five confirmed and four probables. White 576 has a field-applied scheme, with field-modified national insignia. The aircraft lacks the curved glazing aft of the canopy.

20

F4U-1 white 93/BuNo 17430 of Capt Edwin L Olander, VMF-214, Vella Lavella/Torokina, January 1944

Olander flew a shuttle mission from Vella Lavella

to Torokina on 5 January 1944 in this machine. The aircraft wears a field-applied three-tone scheme and updated national insignia.

21
F4U-1A white 740/BuNo 17740 of Maj Gregory Boyington, CO of VMF-214, Vella Lavella, December 1943

Boyington commanded VMF-214 from 7 September 1943 until he was shot down and captured on 3 January 1944. During that time he was credited with 22 aircraft destroyed and 4 probables. His unit carried out the first fighter sweep against Rabaul, a tactic aimed at destroying as many Japanese fighters as possible. The 'Black Sheep' were credited with 126 aircraft destroyed, 34 probables and 6 damaged. Following its service in the South Pacific, the unit returned to the US where it trained for carrier ops. On 18 March 1945 it commenced operations again on board the USS *Franklin*, but was put out of the war the next day when the ship was bombed and had to retire.

22
F4U-1A white 883/BuNo 17883 of Maj Gregory Boyington, CO of VMF-214, Vella Lavella, December 1943

Both Boyington and 1st Lt Robert W McClurg flew this aircraft on numerous occasions.

23
F4U-1A white 86 *Lulubelle*/BuNo 18086 of Maj Gregory Boyington, CO of VMF-214, Vella Lavella, December 1943

Although VMF-214 did not have any aircraft assigned to it, this F4U is marked with 20 of Boyington's kills, as well as having both the name *Lulubelle* and the Major's details painted on it.

24
FG-1A white 271/BuNo 13271 of Maj Julius W Ireland, VMF-211, Bougainville, January 1944

Ireland claimed two Zeros whilst flying '271' on a sweep to Rabaul on 23 January 1944. Earlier that day, while escorting SBDs to the same target, he had downed another Zero and a probable while flying F4U-1 BuNo 17586. Prior to that, on the 3rd (in F4U-1 BuNo 17526) Ireland got a Zero over Rabaul, and on the 17th (in F4U-1 BuNo 17924) claimed a third-share of a Zero with Capt Winfree and Lt Paradis. Ireland brought his final tally to 5.333 on the 29th (in FG-1A BuNo 13259) when he downed a Zero whilst escorting B-24s to Rabaul.

25
F4U-1A white 17-F-13 of Lt(jg) James A Halford, VF-17, USS *Bunker Hill*, August 1943

Halford got his 3.5 kills in the Wildcat in 1942.

26
F4U-1A white 1 *BIG HOG*/BuNo 17649 of Lt Cdr

John T Blackburn, CO VF-17, Ondonga, November 1943

Blackburn claimed 11 kills, 5 probables and 3 damaged whilst CO of VF-17. His outfit was one of the most successful in the Solomons, claiming a total of 154.5 confirmed victories. Unlike Marine units, it also assigned F4Us to individual pilots.

27
F4U-1A white 19 of Lt Paul Cordray, VF-17, Ondonga, November 1943

Cordray claimed seven aircraft destroyed, one probable and three damaged

28
F4U-1A white 15 of Lt(jg) Daniel G Cunningham, VF-17, Ondonga, February 1944

Cunningham scored seven kills and 1.5 damaged.

29
F4U-1A white 9 *LONESOME POLECAT* of Lt Merl W Davenport, VF-17, Ondonga, January 1944

'Butch' Davenport claimed 6.25 aircraft destroyed.

30
F4U-1A white 34 *L.A. CITY LIMITS*/BuNo 17932 of Lt(jg) Doris C Freeman, VF-17, Ondonga, November 1943

'Chico' Freeman claimed two aircraft destroyed and two probables with VF-17, before going on to claim another seven kills with VF-84 in 1945.

31
F4U-1A white 29 of Lt(jg) Ira C Kepford, VF-17, Bougainville, January 1944

'Ike' Kepford was the Navy's most successful Corsair pilot with 16 confirmed victories, 1 probable and 1 damaged.

32
F4U-1A white 29 of Lt(jg) Ira C Kepford, VF-17, Bougainville, January 1944

Kepford's second white 29 wears his final tally. Unlike his first F4U (written off in a crash-landing in January 1943), this machine wore a scoreboard on both sides of the fuselage.

33
F4U-1 white 9/BuNo 02288 of Maj Gregory J Weissenberger, CO of VMF-213, Guadalcanal, June 1943

Weissenberger claimed five Zeros, the first three on 30 June 1943 and the remaining two on 11 and 18 July. White 9 was his usual mount, and was finished in the standard two-tone scheme. Walkways are bordered in black on the upper surface of the wings, and each gunport is covered with three strips of tape.

34
F4U-1A white 17/BuNo 18005 of Lt Cdr Roger R

Hedrick, VF-17, Bougainville, March 1944
Hedrick gained his last three victories with VF-17 in this F4U on 18 February 1944. Earlier, a trio of kills had been scored in BuNos 17659 and 55798.

35
F4U-1A white 25 of Lt Harry A March, Jr, VF-17, Bougainville, May 1944
March gained the status of ace by shooting down two Zeros on 28 January 1944, adding to his previous three kills gained with VF-6 during August 1942 flying the Wildcat.

36
F4U-1A white 9 of Lt(jg) Earl May, VF-17, Bougainville, January 1944
May claimed eight confirmed victories, all Zeros.

37
F4U-1A white 22 of Ens John M Smith, VF-17, Bougainville, February 1944
Smith claimed three aircraft destroyed, three probables and one damaged with VF-17, and later claimed seven victories with VF-84 in 1945.

38
F4U-1A white 3 of Ens Frederick J Streig, VF-17, February 1944
Streig claimed five aircraft destroyed and two damaged. This F4U is depicted after his last kills – 2.5 Zekes claimed over Rabaul on 27 January 1944. It is unusual in that it retains the red surround to the national insignia, a colour that only appeared with the addition of white bars on 28 June 1943 – the surround was discontinued as of 31 July due to possible confusion with the enemy's *Hinomaru*.

39
F4U–1A white 5/BuNo 17656 of Lt(jg) Thomas Killefer, VF-17, Bougainville, February 1944
Killefer was not an ace but did claim 4.5 aircraft destroyed. He force landed on Nissan Island in this machine following engine failure on 5 March 1944.

40
F4U-2 black 212 *Midnite Cocktail* of Capt Howard W Bollman, VMF(N)-532, Kagman Field, Saipan, April 1944
Bollman intercepted and destroyed a *Betty* at 0112 on 14 April 1944 while flying this machine, which was assigned to Lts Caniff and Reuter. Just prior to Bollman's score, 1st Lt Bonner claimed a *Betty* probable at 0036 and 1st Lt Sovik a third *Betty* confirmed at 0111. These were the unit's only kills. F4U-2 black 212 wears a two-tone scheme. Mods fitted to this F4U included the small generator air scoop on the forward fuselage, starboard wing radome blister and the addition of a VHF whip antenna on the spine, the standard antenna mast having been removed. The canopy is equipped with extra armour plating.

41
FG-1A yellow 056 *Mary*/BuNo 14056 of Capt Francis E Pierce, Jr, VMF-121, Peleliu, November 1944
Of 'Effie' Pierce's six victories and one probable, only one was scored whilst flying the F4U – a *Betty* on 30 June 1943. His previous kills were all in F4Fs. The white area on the fin of this FG-1 served as a unit marking.

42
F4U-1A white 108 of Maj George L Hollowell, VMF-111, Guadalcanal November 1943
Hollowell achieved all his victories while flying the Wildcat with VMF-224, but had his Corsair marked up with his score, together with 25 bomb symbols. The aircraft is finished in the three-tone scheme.

43
F4U-1A black 77/NZ5277, RNZAF, Solomons, 1945
This aircraft wears an irate *Donald Duck* motif and a variety of mission marks and kill tallies, including symbols for nine large bombs, eleven small bombs, nine trucks and eight ships. It is finished in Ocean Blue with Light Grey undersides. The RNZAF roundel has been applied over the previous US insignia, and is slightly offset from the bars. This F4U-1A was brought on charge on 5 May 1944, arriving at Guadalcanal on the 20th. It served with a variety of units before being returned to New Zealand in October 1945. Whilst in the frontline it flew with No 15 Sqn/No 1 SU (Guadalcanal), No 15 Sqn/No 25 SU and No 2 SU (Bougainville), No 15 Sqn/No 2 SU (Torokina), No 14 Sqn/No 30 SU (Guadalcanal), No 16 Sqn/No 30 SU and No 21 Sqn/No 30 SU (both Nissan Island), and finally No 21 Sqn/No 30 SU (Jacquinot Bay).

44
F4U-1A white 122 of VMF-111, Gilbert Islands, 1944
White 122, decorated with 100 mission marks, was the only aeroplane to receive an official citation during the war. The Corsair was designed as a fighter, but was used in the ground attack role to great effect. At first field mods were made to allow the aircraft to carry bombs, then Chance Vought responded by producing F4Us capable of fulfilling the role. It was this versatility that ensured the Corsair's longevity after World War 2.

45
Corsair II white TRH/JT427 of Maj Ronald C Hay, RM, No 47 Wg, HMS *Victorious*, January 1945
Hay shot down an *Oscar* and a *Tojo* on 24 January 1945 in this aircraft – on the 29th he again shared in the destruction of an *Oscar* and a *Tojo*. It is painted in Dark Sea Grey and Dark Sea Green over Light Grey. His aircraft was fitted with field-installed oblique and vertical cameras in the lower port fuselage. Delivered to the Navy in August

1944, JT427 was written off when it suffered a landing accident aboard *Victorious* in May 1945, its pilot, Sub Lt R L White (RNZN), escaping unhurt as the fighter came to rest on the deck edge.

46
Corsair II white T8H/JT410 of Sub Lt Donald J Sheppard, RCNVR, No 1836 Sqn, HMS *Victorious*, January 1945

Sheppard was the only FAA pilot to reach the status of ace having gained all his victories in the Corsair. He downed two *Oscars* and a *Tojo* on 4 January 1945, the latter being listed as a probable although it may later have been confirmed, and on the 29th he shared in the destruction of an *Oscar* and a *Tojo* with Maj Hay – all of these scores were achieved in this aircraft. On 4 May, whilst flying Corsair II JT537, he downed a *Judy*, thus becoming an ace. JT410 had been delivered to the Navy in July, and was badly damaged during a heavy landing by Sub Lt Holland (RNZN) on 9 February 1945, resulting in it being declared Category X with both main wheels broken off. It was repaired at Bankstown, Australia, in June 1945, but its subsequent fate is unknown. Prior to Sheppard gaining kills in JT410, Lt J B Edmundson, also of No 1836 Sqn, used it to shoot down an *Oscar* off Car Nicobar on 19 October 1944.

47
F4U-1D white 1 of Maj Herman H Hansen, Jr, VMF-112, USS *Bennington*, February 1945

Hansen claimed a Zero on 30 June 1943 whilst CO of VMF-122. He re-opened his scoring on 17 February 1945 when he shot down an *Oscar* over Hara-machida, Japan, and then went on to destroy another 3.5 aircraft and damage 2.5. His F4U is adorned with *Bennington*'s 'Pine Tree' geometric recognition symbol, as used in early 1945. Part of the 'G' system that came into force on 27 January 1945, these markings were intended to simplify unit recognition with the large number of carriers operating together. However, they proved difficult to recognise and describe, and were replaced by a block letter system introduced in July.

48
F4U-1D white 167/BuNo 57803 of Lt Cdr Roger R Hedrick, VF-84, USS *Bunker Hill*, February 1945

Hedrick destroyed 2 Franks and a Zero on 25 February 1945 whilst flying this machine to bring his final score to 12 aircraft destroyed and 4 damaged. It is shown as it appeared at the time of his kills, having had its temporary yellow nose band (employed on the first Tokyo raids) painted over. The F4U has the vertical arrow 'G' symbol.

49
F4U-1D white 184 of Lt Willis G Laney, VF-84, USS *Bunker Hill*, February 1945

Laney claimed two Zeros and a probable on the same mission that Hedrick claimed his last kills on 25 February over Inubo Point, in the Katori airfield area, Japan. Laney was credited with five aircraft destroyed, two probables and one damaged.

50
F4U-1D white 66 flown by Ens Alfred Lerch, VF-10, USS *Intrepid*, April 1945

Lerch claimed six *Nates* and a *Val* on 16 April in this F4U, which displays *Intrepid*'s 'G' symbol. VF-10 was the only unit to use the F4F, F6F and F4U in combat, its three tours producing 27 aces.

51
F4U-1D yellow FF-59 flown by Lt Col Donald K Yost, CO of VMF-351, USS *Cape Gloucester*, July 1945

Yost gained six kills in the F4F with VMF-121, and later added to his score by downing a *Judy* and a *Francis* on 23 July and 5 August 1945 respectively, bringing his tally to eight. Yost led the MAG aboard the *Cape Gloucester*, being one of the first F4U units to enter combat aboard an escort carrier.

52
F4U-1D white 6 of Lt Joe D Robbins, VF-85, USS *Shangri-La*, December 1944

VF-85 boarded *Shangri-La* on 11 November 1944 for a six-week shakedown. On arrival at San Diego they were re-equipped with 36 new cannon-armed F4U-1C, which were flown into combat. Robbins did, however, fly both F4U-1Ds and FG-1Ds in combat. He became the only ace to serve with VF-85, adding three kills to his previous F6F claims.

53
F4U-1C white 11 of Lt Joe D Robbins, VF-85, USS *Shangri-La*, May 1945

Robbins downed three Zeros and damaged a fourth whilst flying F4U-1C BuNo 82574 on 11 May 1945. He claimed his previous kills while serving with VF-6 on USS *Intrepid*. He shot down a *Topsy* on 29 January 1944 while flying F6F-3 BuNo 66010 and a Zero on 16 February in F6F-3 BuNo 40027. This F4U-1C wears the lightning bolt symbol that was assigned to the *Shangri-La* in January 1945.

54
F4U-1D white 51 flown by 1st Lt Robert Wade, VMF-323, Okinawa, May 1945

Wade claimed seven kills – two *Tonys* on 15 April 1945, two *Vals*, two *Nates* and three *Nates* damaged on 4 May, 0.5 of a *Dinah* on 12 May and 0.5 of a *Val* on 3 June.

55
F4U-1D white 8/BuNo 57413 of 1st Lt Jack Broering, VMF-323, Espiritu Santo, October 1944 to March 1945

Broering was assigned this aircraft while VMF-323 was at Espiritu, the unit not continuing the practice of assigning aircraft to pilots following the move to Okinawa. Broering didn't get the opportunity to gain any kills as he was 'never in the right place at the right time'. He, along with the rest of VMF-323, flew endless CAPs and ground attack missions.

56
F4U-1D white 31 of 1st Lt Francis A Terrill, VMF-323, Okinawa, May 1945
Terrill claimed 6.083 destroyed and 4 damaged between 15 April and 17 May 1945.

57
F4U-1D white 26 of 1st Lt Jerimaiah J O'Keefe, VMF-323, Okinawa, April 1945
O'Keefe downed five *Vals* on 22 April and two *Nates* on the 28th, all *kamikazes*.

58
F4U-1D white 207 of 2nd Lt Marvin S Bristow, VMF-224, Okinawa, May 1945
Although Bristow's F4U is adorned with three kill marks, he has only ever been credited with 1.5, these being a Zero and 0.5 of a *Kate* on 4 and 6 May 1945, respectively. The unit placed their aircraft numbers aft of the cowl flaps, the yellow prop boss serving as a squadron marking.

59
F4U-4 white 13/BuNo 80879 of Capt Kenneth A Walsh, VMF-222, Okinawa, June 1945
Walsh claimed his last kill – a Zero piloted by a *kamikaze* – on 22 June 1945 in this aircraft.

60
F4U-1D white F-107 of 1st Lt Phillip C DeLong, VMF-913, MCAS Cherry Point, North Carolina 1944
DeLong, like many F4U aces returned to the US and joined Training Command to pass on his combat experience. While serving at Cherry Point he had this aircraft adorned with his full score. DeLong was later posted to VMF-312 aboard USS *Bataan* during the Korean War, where he downed two Yak-9s during a recce mission on 21 April 1951 whilst flying F4U-4 BuNo 97380 – for further details see *Aircraft of the Aces 4 - Korean War Aces*.

FIGURE PLATES

1
Capt Arthur R 'Rog' Conant of VMF-215 at Torokina in January 1944. He is wearing typical 'garb' for a USMC/Navy Corsair fighter pilot in the Pacific, namely Marine Corps issue khaki shirt and trousers, a personalised US Navy lightweight flying jacket and 'Boondocker' field boots. His M40 helmet and Wilson Mk 2 goggles are also standard issue, as is the throat microphone. Conant has his parachute and survival pack slung over one shoulder, and an N2885 life preserver, equipped with a dye marker and whistle, around his other arm. Finally, around his waist Conant wears an M1936 pistol belt to which he has attached a holstered Colt 1911A1 .45 cal pistol and a pouch for magazine clips. His gloves and sunglasses are standard Navy issue.

2
Capt Harold L Spears (15 victories and 3 probables), also of VMF-215, at Bougainville in December 1943. Showing a rather more casual approach to combat flying gear than most of his contemporaries, Spears is wearing a 'cut down' pair of USMC khaki trousers and a long-sleeve shirt. Having dispensed with his boots, Spears usually flew in this dusty pair of privately-purchased suede 'desert boots'. His headgear is very much regulation issue, however, and is identical to that worn by squadron-mate Conant. Spears' life-jacket is also an N2885, but he is wearing it back to front – a common trait inexplicably perpetrated by many pilots.

3
Maj Gregory 'Pappy' Boyington at Vella Lavella in December 1943. Again wearing much the same clothing as Conant and Spears, 'Pappy's' one distinguishing feature is his early-issue life preserver, 'borrowed' from VMF-122.

4
Cigar-smoking 1st Lt John F Bolt, Jr, was also a 'Black Sheep' at Vella Lavella in early 1944. His uniform is standard issue, aside from the customised earphones within his helmet. He has also partially inflated his life-jacket, a practice adopted by a number of pilots in-theatre.

5
Although flying Corsairs with the Royal Navy's FAA from HMS *Victorious* in early 1945, Royal Marine Maj Ronnie Hay is wearing a US Navy-style one-piece lightweight overall, which was the favoured item of clothing within the BPF's flying community. His 'Mae West' is a late-war pattern issue, with additional pockets containing survival equipment. Hay is carrying a Type C helmet fitted with a late-war mask and Mk VIII goggles. Finally, he is wearing standard-issue patent leather shoes.

6
Lt Harry A 'Dirty Eddie' March, Jr, of VF-17 at Bougainville in May 1944. He is wearing US Navy/Marine Corps herringbone twill coveralls and 'Boondockers', with a leather waist belt and a Colt 1911A1 .45 cal pistol attached. His early-pattern life-vest has a survival kit (in white) slung underneath it, the former also carrying his name emblazoned across the front. Finally, his helmet and mask are very much late-war issue, compared with other USMC pilots profiled on this spread.